MORE THAN 65 NOTABLE ACHIEVERS ON HOW
TO MAKE THE MOST OF THE REST OF YOUR LIFE

65

THINGS TO DO
WHEN YOU RETIRE

Edited by Mark Evan Chimsky

Associate Project Editor: Renee Rooks Cooley

SELLERS
PUBLISHING

Published by Sellers Publishing, Inc.

Copyright © 2012 Sellers Publishing, Inc.
All rights reserved.

Sellers Publishing, Inc.
161 John Roberts Road, South Portland, Maine 04106
Visit our Web site: www.sellerspublishing.com • E-mail: rsp@rsvp.com

Design by Faceout Studio

ISBN 13: 978-1-4162-0654-5
e-ISBN: 978-1-4162-0736-8
Library of Congress Control Number: 2011935637

10 9 8 7 6 5 4 3 2

Printed in the United States of America.

Credits: page 399

CONTENTS

SECTION 3
Do Good By Giving Back

SECTION 4
How Working in Retirement Can Work for You

Section 5
A New Freedom to Be Yourself

Section 6
Family Matters

Section 7
Go for It!

INTRODUCTION

Welcome to the new world of retirement! Consider 65 *Things to Do When You Retire* your user's manual to making the most of the years ahead. Many retirement guides contain tips and ideas by one or two authors, but we thought, *why not provide readers with wisdom and practical advice from more than 65 notable contributors, including experts on the subject as well as achievers in their 60s who have forged unusual and fulfilling paths?*

In selecting the contributors for this book, one of our goals was to be as wide-ranging and inclusive as possible, to reveal all the wonderful possibilities that can make retirement rewarding. You'll read true stories of people in retirement who sought meaningful new jobs and volunteer opportunities — like Rick Koca, who tells his uplifting story of starting the nonprofit StandUp For Kids, and Bob Lowry, who shares his dramatic account of working in prison ministry. And there are lively personal essays of achievement by Ruth Heidrich, who won a gold medal in the Senior Olympics; Leigh Anne Jasheway, who teaches stand-up comedy; and Stephanie Cowell, who is pursuing her passion to be a novelist.

We have included essays on how to make the most of retirement, now that it's arrived (see essays by Sydney Lagier and John E. Nelson, for example); how to reclaim — or discover — your purpose or passions (see what Gloria Steinem, Ernie Zelinski, and Sally Paradysz, among others, have to say); how to adjust to retirement when you have to take a spouse or partner's needs into consideration (see the essays by Dave D'Antoni and Dorian Mintzer); and how to develop smart financial strategies (as discussed by Anna Rappaport, Mark Cussen, Jim Yih, Julie Jason, and Aaron Smith). We even offer up a lighthearted look at retirement by famous cartoonist Mort Gerberg. And last but not least, we are especially honored to be able to include an essay by former President Jimmy Carter. He and his wife, Rosalynn, have taught us by their example how to create a productive and life-affirming retirement by being involved citizens of the world.

It is our hope that this "roadmap to retirement" will inspire you to dust off dreams that may have been long deferred and to follow your bliss in ways that you didn't even think possible. Remember, the best is yet to come!

Section

REDEFINING
RETIREMENT

Don't Let Retirement Steal Your Bliss!

by Robert Delamontagne

Robert Delamontagne is the author of *The Retiring Mind: How to Make the Psychological Transition to Retirement* and *Honey, I'm Home: How to Prevent or Resolve Marriage Conflicts Caused by Retirement*. He is the founder and retired chairman of EduNeering Inc. (now Kaplan EduNeering). He earned his Ph.D. in educational psychology from Georgia State University. He currently resides with his wife, Sherrilyn, in New Hope, Pennsylvania, and Marco Island, Florida. He may be contacted at www.theretiringmind.com.

W hen I retired at the age of 63, I thought I was well prepared for this new stage of life. I sold the company I had founded and managed for 25 years, and at long last I had achieved financial security.

But it came as a shock to me when I discovered that I was not really prepared for my retirement on an emotional level. It should not have come as a surprise, considering that I had lived my life in a very intense and structured way for 35 years and then one day all that familiar structure and mental stimulation were gone. As a result I began experiencing intense irritability and emotional stress. It seemed to get worse over time, and I realized that I needed to get to the bottom of my problem, and quick.

Why didn't anyone warn me that retirement often requires a major psychological adjustment on the same level as the death of a loved one or a bitter divorce? When I began asking friends and acquaintances if they had experienced this problem, I learned to my great surprise that many of them had suffered through a very difficult and painful period after retirement, particularly if the termination of their employment had not been of their own choosing but that of their employer.

I also learned that most were embarrassed to talk about it, because, in most people's minds, retirement is supposed to be a glorious time of freedom from stress and the normal demands of life. This can also be a very dangerous time for many people because they become susceptible to making life-altering mistakes in order to alleviate stress, such as selling their house and moving to a new location, buying a second home, making poor investments, getting a divorce, or self-medicating with alcohol or drugs.

As I continued to search for the source of my problem, I began talking to more and more people about how they experienced their transition to retirement. I discovered that many who had encountered the greatest difficulty had had very successful careers and suffered from achievement addiction. During their careers, they received a great deal of positive rewards (monetary and emotional) because they were very good at their jobs. Over the years, they began to need this positive feedback as an essential aspect of their existence.

In effect, a large part of their identities were job-related. They defined themselves by *what* they did, not *who* they were as people. So for them, retirement represented a subconscious loss of their sense of self.

I immediately realized that this was the primary cause of my emotional distress. A very large part of my identity was being the CEO and chairman of the company I had founded. I saw everything through the prism of the business and what I needed to do to ensure its success. Over time, my very identity became infused with the role I played running the business. I did not see myself as a person independent from what I did for a living — it had defined me.

It is not a stretch to realize the magnitude of this challenge. It requires a redefinition of the self, but also a rediscovery of the very essence or core of one's being. For many, retirement is a time for personal growth, which becomes the path to greater personal freedom.

Here are five steps you can take to help you successfully transition into retirement:

1. **Know your personality type.** The very personality characteristics that supported your career success can work against you in retirement. If you tend to be a perfectionist or a dominant personality, you are more likely to encounter emotional and marital problems when you retire. The greater your self-understanding, the more you will be able to modulate self-defeating behavioral tendencies.

2. **Find activities that are an expression of your unique personality type.** One size does not fit all in retirement.

Your unique personality determines those things that bring positive energy into your life. If you can identify those activities that feel natural and pleasurable, you will start down a path that brings joy to yourself and others.

3. **Have someone you can talk to.** In the event you encounter strong negative emotions after your retirement, you will need someone who will listen attentively while you share your feelings. There is absolutely no substitute for a spouse or close personal friend who will support you and help you through this stressful period. If no one is available, then counseling may be the best course of action.

4. **Make no major decisions during the adjustment period.** People who suffer adjustment problems after their retirement often make poor decisions in an attempt to cope with their negative feelings. No major decisions should be made until a new and healthy equilibrium has been established.

5. **Make sure your personal beliefs support your happiness.** Many people feel that their lives are over once they retire. As Malcolm Forbes said, "Retirement kills more people than hard work ever did." It is

essential that you possess a positive mental outlook. This may be a core set of spiritual beliefs or simply a sense that life is supportive of your innermost desires. These beliefs function as scaffolding that will support your transition.

Retirement sets in motion a psychological reconciliation and accommodation process that is natural and life-supporting. Give this process time to work. It can take as long as three years to completely adjust to your retirement. Be patient and know that a new life is awakening within you.

2

Rewire® Early and Often

by Jeri Sedlar and Rick Miners

Jeri Sedlar and Rick Miners, a husband and wife consulting team, are coauthors of *Don't Retire, REWIRE!*® 5 *Steps to Fulfilling Work That Fuels Your Passion, Suits Your Personality, and Fills Your Pocket.* They are the creators of the concept of rewiring® and rewirement®. Sedlar is a nationally recognized speaker and the senior advisor at the Conference Board on the Mature Workforce. Miners was cofounder of FlexCorp Systems, a business process outsourcing company that had 1,000 employees, including 300 retirees who came back to work. He sold his company in 2006. They travel the country speaking and consulting on transition and personal growth. Their Web site is www.dontretirerewire.com.

The new reality is that we will probably be living longer, healthier, and younger lives with less money than we anticipated. Given that, it becomes critical that people figure out what makes them tick — at work, at play, in life overall, so they will use their time, energy, and money well in the future. We've always believed this, but it is even more important today.

The first edition of our book *Don't Retire, REWIRE!®* 5 *Steps to Fulfilling Work That Fuels Your Passion, Suits Your Personality, and Fills Your Pocket* was published in 2002 and the second edition in 2007. But it was in the late 1990s when we first got the idea for the book. We started to meet people of all ages who wanted to cash out their corporate stock options so they could retire early. We were intrigued and asked them why they wanted to retire. We heard a variety of reasons, including: "Because we can," "We hit our "number," or "Why not?" Everyone seemed to be predicating their future on "their money." Society's big question about retirement has always been, "Do you have enough money to retire?" and these people were playing right into society's expectations. We were executive recruiters at the time, dealing with candidates and clients, and we knew that people were far more complex than they realized. We knew that money contributed to people's happiness, but we also knew how important fulfillment was to the happiness equation.

We went further and asked, "Now that you have enough money to retire, what do you want to do?" After getting the expected answers about traveling, volunteering, and spending time with grandchildren, we decided a tougher question was needed. We then asked, "Now that you have enough money to retire, what do you want to do that will fulfill you?" We received blank stares from most of the 300-plus people we interviewed, and so we knew we were onto something. It was not surprising that in this fast-paced world, most people don't take the time to know themselves. In fact, most people fail to recognize the places, people, and activities that give them joy and enhance their lives. After much research, we concluded that most people suffered from a lack of self-knowledge. We decided that "knowing what fulfills you" should be the foundation of *Don't Retire, REWIRE!* and the cornerstone of life planning. To help people get smarter about themselves, we created the concept of rewiring® and the five-step rewiring process.

Our belief is that before people transition into their next act, or decide what to do in the future, they need to take the time to figure out what motivates and fulfills them. The truth is, the better you know yourself, the better the choices you'll make in the future, and that's where the rewiring® process comes in.

Rewiring® vs. Retiring

We like to say that "you retire from . . . and you rewire® to . . . " Rewiring® is about taking the energy normally given to traditional work and rerouting it into new activities — but the key is to select activities that will fulfill you, not just keep you busy or fill your time. There is a big difference between being fulfilled and just being busy. The rewiring® process is both mental and physical, and includes attitude and actions. A key factor for a successful rewiring® is to be open to seeing yourself and opportunities in a whole new way.

Discovering What Makes You Tick

Many people don't realize what they get from work beyond a paycheck until they are no longer working. In doing research for *Don't Retire, REWIRE!*® we asked pre- and post-retirees, who did either paid or volunteer work, the question, "Why do you — or why did you — work beyond a paycheck?" We were stunned to receive a total of 85 candid reasons that we called *drivers*. The drivers ran the gamut from having the desire to belong, to be creative, and to have accomplishments; "esteem" drivers included reasons having to do with being valued, having power, and being a leader.

In essence, drivers are our motivators, our personal DNA. They consciously or subconsciously direct us to make the decisions and choices we do. Drivers can impact or influence all of the aspects of our lives. Identifying and understanding our drivers is essential to creating a future that is fulfilling and emotionally and physically rewarding.

Mistakes Happen

Unfortunately, we have seen people begin to build a future based on other people's dreams or recommendations, which can lead to disappointment, frustration, even loss of money. A woman we know told us that helping the homeless was a primary interest of hers, and that making a difference was her #1 driver — followed by being a leader and being creative. She initially thought that she would be a hands-on volunteer in a soup kitchen, feeding the homeless — but in the rewiring process she identified her drivers and discovered that pursuing a volunteer leadership and administrative role with an organization that feeds the homeless would be more *fulfilling* to her in the long term than actually working in the soup kitchen.

Both roles are important, but we need to listen to our drivers and allow them to direct us in finding fulfilling new activities that are enjoyable and sustainable.

Freedom Needs to Be Managed

Creating a rewired® life portfolio takes on a greater importance when you are faced with a potentially empty calendar. We know people who suffer from "fear of the white space" once they retire. They manifest their fear by committing to things before asking themselves, "Is this really what I want to do?" As a result, the commitment becomes burdensome, less enjoyable, and short-lived. We view a rewired® life portfolio as one that is balanced between work, play, family, community, and self, and includes a good dose of meaning and purpose.

The rewiring® process is fun and straightforward and will help you to identify not only your drivers, but who and what you want in your life. It's true that the economy may remain volatile, the job market challenging, and constant change might become the "new normal," but by learning the rewiring® process, you'll create a lifeline to fulfillment and fun for the rest of your life.

3

Retire "Retirement" . . . Build Your "Life Portfolio" Instead

by Michael Jeans

Michael D. Jeans is president of New Directions, Inc., a nationally recognized career-management firm in Boston that helps senior executives and professionals develop new jobs, start new ventures, and find alternatives to full-time employment (or full-time retirement). Previously, Jeans was president and CEO of Roxy.com, Inc., an online retailer of consumer electronics. Earlier, he was CEO of Nashua Photo, Inc., and president of Wesson/Peter Pan Foods (a division of Conagra). He has a B.A. from the College of the Holy Cross, *magna cum laude* and an MBA from the Tuck School of Business at Dartmouth College. Jeans is a director of AMICA Mutual Insurance Company. He also serves on the Board of Directors of the Boys & Girls Club of Greater Nashua (New Hampshire) and the Boston Minuteman Council of the Boy Scouts of America.

Most people can now expect to live longer. Those extra years are a great gift. But they can be albatrosses if people don't know what to do with them. Some people like to stay the course, whatever it is. But most people find that they need to dig down to their core selves and discover new goals and purposes that touch something deep inside — the pursuits that get them out of bed in the morning.

One year after he retired, a gentleman with a 30-year career at a Fortune 500 company was heard to say, "You have to be original, and it's not easy. There's no falling back on what you've done. It's like learning how to play golf left-handed when you've been a righty all your life."

When you "retire," you're on your own. No longer is most of your life ahead. You don't have forever to fulfill promises. But there's also good news: Now, going forward, can be the most important part of your life, when it all comes together — your experience, wisdom, and successes. Now is when you ask: *What was it all for? How will I tell at journey's end that I have not just visited this world, but have lived a full life?*

This time, it's about you, your family, and sharing your good fortune with others. The only imperatives are within: your values and dreams, priorities and principles. Your new mission is recognizing those drivers, discovering what matters to you, and pursuing your life on your terms.

But you face challenges and unknown territory. There's no map, few models, and scant reliable advice to guide you. You have to look inward for clues. It isn't easy. You cannot just hope that life will take care of itself, that what got you here will get you the rest of the way. This is no time to wing it, to coast to the finish line. It's time to be intentional, to take control of your life on new terms.

Let's Retire the Word "Retirement"

Consider the word "retirement." It comes from *tirer*, French for "pull" or "draw." Add the Latin prefix *re* (back), and it means "to retreat, draw back, or pull back" — like pulling a punch or drawing the wagons in a circle.

"To retire" originally meant to leave, recede, or cease activity; to step down, give up, or go away. Retirement suggests what we don't do (work), not what we do do! It is passive. We retire from something. Hemingway called it "the ugliest word in the English language."

Retirement is getting a makeover these days. There's un-, anti-, and semi-retirement, revolving retirement, "refirement," and "re-aspirement." But just changing the word doesn't work. Shuffleboard at a "rekindlement" community is still shuffleboard. Let's forget the verbal salvage attempts and put "retirement" to pasture.

It Is Time for Your "Life Portfolio"

Life spans have increased and will continue to edge upward, with older Americans becoming more vigorous. That has yielded a new life stage — the first new stage since social scientists identified adolescence a century ago — extending middle age anywhere from age 50 to 90.

Previous approaches to retirement are obsolete in light of this change, and we have fresh opportunities to make this new stage meaningful. The way to do this is to adopt a life-planning model called a "life portfolio."

The word "portfolio" describes this new model well. *Port-folio* first meant a leather carrying case of important documents: a portable book. It later came to mean something that represents your work, interests, or accomplishments — in short, something that reflects all of who you are, not just the career you.

In finance, a portfolio contains invested assets allocated

into diversified sectors. It takes wisdom, skill, and a sense of perspective to balance a portfolio well.

Like a collection of stocks and bonds, your own "life portfolio" is an integrated mix of personal holdings or assets. It covers the gifts, values, passions, and pursuits that make you who you are.

A life portfolio is an agenda for living that we always carry with us. It's a balanced mix of activities that matter to and motivate you. It's a design for living from the inside out — your life, your way.

A life portfolio is the central theme of our existence, the values-driven agenda we will always have with us. A career has a shelf life; a life portfolio is ageless.

Build Your Own Life Portfolio

A life portfolio offers a compelling alternative to traditional retirement. It is a new way of thinking and living in extended middle age. A typical portfolio is a balanced mix of some work, ongoing learning, recreation, travel and avocations, reconnecting with family and friends, and giving back. It's an agenda for turning careers to callings.

How do you do it? No single path suits everyone.

Portfolios are planned months or years in advance, or they may arise from sudden events that require you to make a new plan or adapt previous ones on the fly. Life portfolios are sometimes possible within current organizations as people take on new, more flexible, and less stressful responsibilities.

Some life portfolio paths that people have created include: serving on a board of directors; leading or volunteering for a nonprofit; starting/acquiring a business or practice; investing in emerging ventures; consulting; coaching; writing; teaching; public speaking; mentoring young people; ongoing learning or seeking advanced degrees; turning hobbies into income; performing public service; or even creating legacies by writing personal memoirs or family histories.

People who embrace the life portfolio concept are men and women who want to continue leading a life of significance, while also taking time to rest, recharge, and enjoy the fruits of their labor. They know that the essence of happiness is fulfilling their unique and full potential at all stages of their lives.

And yes, some even learn to swing left-handed.

4

New Models for Success

by David C. Borchard, Ed.D., NCC

David Borchard, Ed.D., NCC, a professional counselor and coach, has 30 years experience helping individuals identify their passion and create new visions for their lives and work. Working with clients individually, at the World Bank and other settings, he specializes in transition counseling, retirement lifestyle planning, and executive coaching. He's taught graduate-level courses at the Johns Hopkins University and is on the faculty of the federal government's Management Development Center. Borchard is author of *The Joy of Retirement: Finding Happiness, Freedom, and the Life You've Always Wanted* and creator of the Passion Revealer, an online assessment for discovering where one's talents and interests meet new possibilities. Visit him at www.VisionTRAC.com.

To exist is to change; to change is to mature; to mature is to go on creating oneself endlessly. — Henri Bergson

Stop: Before you decide what to do in retirement, reassess what you value most. In doing so, remember that your values today may not be the ones you had in the past or will have in the future.

As a professional counselor and life coach, I see many clients who have recently retired and others who are in transition from full-time employment. The typical presenting issue from these clients is: *"What do I really want to do with the time I have left?"*

At this stage of life, when you have more freedom than ever before, making choices about your future can be exhilarating. But with a world full of possibilities, those same choices can also be overwhelming, especially since the stakes are high. What you choose may have a significant impact on the quality of your life, including your health, longevity, and happiness.

New Guidelines for Success

What is your current measure for personal success? Is it simply getting out of bed another day? Whittling your golf game down to a low handicap? Keeping your retirement kitty full to overflowing? Some define success as setting their own schedule and not reporting to anyone. A friend of mine characterizes the good life as a hot cup of coffee, a newspaper, and a comfortable chair in front of the fireplace.

According to many advertisements geared to seniors, all you really need for the good life is the perfect retirement community — or the one featured in a particular ad. Such a lifestyle may suit you to a tee if you have a passion for golf or bridge. But what if you are unlikely to find fulfillment in an identity based on being a good golfer or a master bridge player?

My personal and professional experience convinces me that a fulfilling lifestyle as a senior depends on developing new criteria for success. This is particularly true if your identity or self-worth stemmed from a professional title or work-related accomplishments. Career success has often equated to life success. But when you leave professional titles and performance evaluations behind, how do you know when you're successful?

Feeling successful and living purposefully is important in any stage of life. But in our youth we depended upon societal expectations and individual responsibilities to guide our choices about things like career development, family lifestyle, and even where to go on vacation. Around 50-something, we graduated from a life dominated by obligations, but we realized that even though we had more choices, we could never pursue them all. Time had become a precious commodity.

Replacing Early Life Structures

As seniors, we need to create new models for success — ones that grow out of new sets of core values. There are various ways of reassessing our values. First and foremost for those of us in a committed relationship is to engage our partner in the process.

We can consult self-help books, therapists, and life coaches, those already retired, or wise crones and gurus. Ultimately, however, there is no substitute for unencumbered self-reflection. After all, you are the only person who actually knows what you really want. The following exercise can help you in your self-reflection. Prioritize your values by using the table on page 33 to:

- Identify categories most essential to your future.

- Number your categories in the left-hand column, from #1 to #17, with #1 being your highest priority, #2 your second highest, etc.

- Define what success looks like to you in each of your *top seven* categories by setting goals for each. (See examples on page 32.)

- Your lowest-rated categories may serve as reminders of what to avoid.

Example:

Priority	My Value Priorities	My Goals for Personal Success
1.	Health and well-being	Maintain my health with yoga twice a week; walk, bike, or jog twice a week; join a meditation group.
2.	Relationship	Marriage: Support my spouse by being a positive, nurturing presence and by finding at least three ways to acknowledge her every day. Family: Create a special occasion each year to bring our adult children and grandchildren together. Friends: Find at least one fun thing each month to do with friends.
3.	Location (climate, access to culture, outdoor activities, etc.)	Select a location where my spouse can pursue her interests in the arts and where I have access to interesting consulting possibilities and lifelong learning at a university.

Establishing Your Criteria for Personal Fulfillment

Priority	My Value Priorities	My Goals for Personal Success
	Personal development	
	Spiritual life	
	Relationship	
	Financial security	
	Hobby/leisure activity	
	Work I enjoy	
	Social contribution	
	Home life	
	Health and well-being	
	Material possessions	
	Travel/recreation	
	Location (climate/access)	
	Autonomy, freedom	
	Personal influence and prominence	
	Living adventurously	
	Pursuing my passion	
	A leisurely lifestyle	
	Other:	

Values can and do change. My wife and I continue to reassess our core values and adjust our models for success. Recently, we debated whether or not I should continue a lucrative consulting practice involving a long commute and a considerable amount of time away from home. The income from this work had supported a comfortable lifestyle in our desired location. But the commute had become tedious and was taking time away from working on my memoirs and my less lucrative but more enjoyable home-based coaching practice. In the final analysis, we realized that the work I enjoyed at home had become a higher value than the financial bonuses entailing the commute. A high priority for my wife was seeing me happy in pursuing my new home-based work, and she made a convincing case for trimming some of our expensive habits. As a result, we are now enjoying the rewards of my having more time to pursue what is most meaningful for me at this stage of my life.

To have the life you value, you have to know what you (and your partner) value. Then, at the end of a day, you can say, "Aah, that was a day well spent."

5

Five Keys to a Creative Retirement: Even When This Means Continuing to Work

by Ronald J. Manheimer, Ph.D.

Ronald J. Manheimer, Ph.D., is the former founding director of the North Carolina Center for Creative Retirement, a lifelong learning, leadership, community service, and research institute at the University of North Carolina Asheville, where he was also research associate professor of philosophy. He is the author of A Map to the End of Time: Wayfarings with Friends and Philosophers, Older Americans Almanac, The Second Middle Age, and other publications on aging, philosophy, and human development. In partial retirement, Manheimer is learning how to take some of the advice he's given to others. His Web site is www.ronmanheimer.com.

A useful analogy for understanding the word "creative" in the phrase "creative retirement" is the concept architects use to describe renovating and repurposing an existing building or home

— "adaptive reuse." The goal is to honor the attractive features, historic style, "good bones," and handsome materials of the structure while updating, renovating, and equipping the building for a new function. We've all seen the abandoned warehouse turned into an attractive condominium or a lively community center, a powerhouse made over into an art museum, a barn turned into an intimate theater. Likewise, when we honor our life experiences, knowledge, and expertise, and explore ways to reinterpret our accomplishments to engage in new ventures, we're practicing "adaptive reuse."

So, with this idea in mind, I want to offer five insights I have gleaned while in the process of both guiding others through retirement decision-making and making the journey myself.

1. **Allowing yourself time and patience.** About one-third of men and 12 percent of women who retire from their breadwinning occupation return to work within six months. Some by choice, others by default. Some people have already figured out a series of next steps before they turn in their office or laboratory keys. For others, disengaging from the workforce is like

being handed a blank notebook and told to write the next chapter of their life. What a creative opportunity! "Great," some people say. "I'm just going to do nothing for a while, and see what happens." With no way to structure daily life, doing nothing quickly becomes boring and debilitating. Anxiety builds and . . . *voila!* You are looking for a part-time job doing anything (but staying at home). So, yes, you do need to be patient with yourself and try not to seize the first thing that comes along, because the creative process (adaptive reuse) requires personal reflection, patience, a lot of hard work, discipline, and openness to the unknown and the uncertain.

2. **Learning to structure doing nothing.** For those individuals who look forward to retirement as a transitional period that may lead to some degree of self-change, the next life incubation period involves passage through a series of stages. But you won't really understand these stages while you're going through them. Only afterward. As the Danish existential philosopher Søren Kierkegaard put it, "We experience life forward and understand it backward." So, to make the best use of a period of being open to new possibilities, you need to have some intermediate

structure and purpose. One way to do this is by signing up for classes at a community college or university to try out new interest areas, update your existing skills, acquire new skills, and meet new people who can stimulate your thinking about the future. Going back to school gives you a little time, structure, and a way to use your mind. You will quickly discover both what appeals to you — and what doesn't — as well as some surprises concerning things you didn't think you would like or would be good at.

Another approach is to find an apprenticeship or volunteer intern opportunity to learn up close. A third activity involves setting up some informal job interviews with HR directors at businesses you think you might like to enter. This will give you practice at applying for a job when there's not a lot at stake. HR staff persons will review your résumé and tell you what you might need in order to qualify as a viable candidate for some position with their company, or they might tell you how, with your skills and experience, you could fit into the company if and when a position does open up.

3. **Considering men (not) working.** The sharp delineation of how retirement transitions vary by gender is blurring.

In research from the North Carolina Center for Creative Retirement's Paths to Creative Retirement workshops, researchers found that professional career women are encountering many of the same challenges as their male counterparts — fear over loss of role identity and power, diminished sense of purpose, decline in *joie de vivre*, and so on. Still, women appear to possess better social engagement skills than men. They are more likely to belong to clubs and civic organizations (or to be inclined to join them), and they have a greater capacity to replace work-related friendships than do men. Lack of purpose, social outlets, and activity structure may lead men to scramble back to the workforce, withdraw into isolating home projects, or sink into escapist activities such as TV watching, Internet surfing, or obsessive perusal of stock market reports. While keeping men busy, these compensatory strategies hardly qualify as steps toward a creative retirement. So, what's the remedy? The goal is to expand social connectivity, purposeful activity, self-esteem through productive engagement, and overall enjoyment of life. Ways to get in motion might include: reading books about men's life transitions, joining a men's group, enrolling in educational classes, scheduling a breakfast or lunch with friends and family members, joining or reactivating membership in volunteer organizations, entering counseling or psychotherapy, seeing a career counselor about finding a meaningful second or third career, and exploring a spiritual practice (especially in groups).

4. Expecting resistance and inertia. Here's what they usually don't tell you in advice books and articles about the creative retirement transition-making process: it can be a pain. If you can remember some of the struggles of adolescence or early parenting or recovery from a physical injury or death of a loved one, then` you know that growing through a major life transition takes time, effort, self-knowledge, help from others, rebuilding activities, faith and trust in one's own capacity for self-renewal, and so on. Writing about self-change, Kierkegaard said, "The *way* is not the problem, the problem *is* the way." By which, the enigmatic Dane meant that in our resistance to self-change (anxiety, stubbornness, fatigue, habituation, blame), we might slowly discover the passage we had been seeking. You have to accept that you're going to be stuck sometimes at a crossroads or bound up by a contradiction. Take the example of choice making, which requires an act of will and self-determination but may also involve letting go of earlier decisions, and putting yourself into a frame of mind of receptivity — which can seem the opposite of willful action. There you are in the paradoxical position of wondering whether to go charging up the mountain or to sit in contemplation under a tree in the surrounding hills. The trick is to do both — *to embrace contradictions.*

5. Encountering resistance from others. There's another kind of resistance to self-change connected to retirement: the reaction of others, such as one's spouse or partner, adult children, family members, friends, and acquaintances. Any or all of these folks might not approve of your search, struggle, experimentations, or occasionally erratic emotional states. When you make changes in your life, you tend to trigger discomfort in others. They, too, have to adjust. And retirement, if you go that route, has a subversive-like quality, especially if you're having too good a time and you go around saying things like, "I wish I had done this five years ago." Or, "I can't believe I was so addicted to working." Statements like these can make other people wonder whether they, too, are overdue for a new venture and that can be disconcerting. Don't be surprised if you get push back from those close to you. Humor them as you gently entice them to enter the journey with you.

6

Will You Pass or Flunk Retirement?

by Nancy K. Schlossberg, Ed.D.

Nancy K. Schlossberg, Ed.D., spent most of her career as a professor of counseling psychology. She taught at Howard University, and Wayne State University, and for 26 years at the University of Maryland, College Park. Schlossberg was the first woman executive at the American Council on Education, where she started the Office of Women in Higher Education. Currently, she is copresident of the consulting firm, TransitionWorks, and professor emerita at the University of Maryland. She has written nine books focusing on mid-life, aging, transitions, and coping, including *Overwhelmed: Coping with Life's Ups and Downs* and her new book, *Revitalizing Retirement*. She and her book, *Retire Smart, Retire Happy*, were the focus of a 90-minute PBS special, *Retire Smart, Retire Happy*.

As Marge considers retirement, she says, "I know I will be a retirement failure. I've been struggling with the 'afterlife' for about five years; indeed, this is the most difficult 'transition' I have experienced, and it seems to be the case with many professional women of our ilk. We don't want to 'roll bandages.' What else is there?"

Marge lived through the deaths of an adult daughter and of a grandson born with lupus. So what makes retirement so challenging when she has already met some of life's most difficult challenges? Marge reflects what many report. She has had a rich, full life, working in a career she loves, raising two children, and being part of a 45-year marriage. Missing from her life — no time for hobbies. Her fears revolve around losing her identity and having no purpose or mission in life.

Retirement Tips

Marge, and others like her, can be helped by listening to advice from those planning to retire and those already retired.

Rename retirement. The word "retirement" connotes retreating. We need a new word to reflect what actually occurs. Retirement is changing gears — leaving one major set of activities and moving toward new adventures and new paths.

Prepare for surprise. Retirement is not one transition; it is a series of transitions. No matter how well you plan, there will be unexpected twists and turns. A newspaper writer was surprised by needing to have emergency heart surgery a week after he retired; one woman, never married, met someone at the senior center and fell in love.

Identify your retirement expectations. The contrast between some blue-collar workers living in a mobile home park and a retired CEO of a Fortune 100 company is instructive. Those living in the mobile park never expected to have two homes where the "girls can shop at the mall and the guys fish whenever they want." They were getting more than expected, whereas the CEO's power began to diminish the moment he retired, to his dismay. He had expected to continue to be seen as a major player.

Discover your retirement path. Are you, or do you want to be, one of the following:

- A *Continuer* — Doing more of the same, but different
- An *Adventurer* — Engaging in something new
- A *Searcher* — Looking for your niche
- An *Easy Glider* — Going with the flow
- An *Involved Spectator* — Caring and learning but no longer a key player

- A *Retreater* — Giving up

Get involved, stay involved. Think about what you always wanted to do, a suppressed passion, a regret. Then try to make it happen. A car mechanic had always dreamed of playing the piano. He saved enough money so that when he retired he bought a piano, took lessons, and became involved in what he now calls "the joy of his life." The activity itself is a matter of individual taste; getting into an activity is what counts.

Balance your psychological portfolio. Look at your psychological assets and figure out ways to replace them or duplicate them. Your psychological portfolio has three major parts: your identity; your relationships with colleagues, partners, friends, neighbors; and your purpose or social capital gained from your work and community involvement.

Increase your retirement coping strategies. Handle retirement more creatively by practicing new coping strategies. If something about retirement is bothering you, ask yourself three questions: Can I change the problem? If not, can I change the way I see the problem? Can I reduce my stress level through meditation, exercise, therapy? The bottom line: It's all about attitude, attitude, attitude.

Be patient. Transitions are a process, not an event. Think of taking a trip: You prepare for the trip, you take the trip, you remember the trip. During this period, your reactions will change. Retirement is like that. You think about it, plan it, and do it. And then comes the period of figuring out who you are and how to "get a life." It will take time, so be patient, knowing that Today Is Not Forever.

Your Retirement Quiz
You will pass retirement if you can:

- Rename retirement as a positive.

- Understand that it will be full of surprises — good and bad.

- Be realistic about your expectations.

- Decide which path(s) to follow.

- Get involved.

- Strengthen your "psychological portfolio" — your identity, your relationships, your sense of purpose.

- Use multiple coping strategies.

- Give it time.

- Remember, you can pass retirement.

This essay appeared in the *Psychology Today* blog, and was reprinted from Nancy Schlossberg's Web site www.transitionsthroughlife.com.

7

Women 50+ Know: How to Redefine Retirement

by the Women of VibrantNation.com

The women of VibrantNation.com are the members of the leading online community for baby boomer women — the place where they connect and support each other on issues unique to life after 50, including fashion, beauty, family, relationships, work, money, and sex. There are 40 million baby boomer women, and VibrantNation.com is where their voices are heard.

The transition from working and/or mothering full-time to *living* full-time isn't always easy, but it can be tremendously rewarding. At VibrantNation.com, the leading online community for women over 50, members connect daily to support one another through the various transitions of midlife — including retirement.

Here is some of the advice that the women of

VibrantNation.com have for other midlife women who want to challenge, rediscover, and reinvent themselves in retirement.

To get the most out of "retirement," plan on continuing to work. "Most of my retired friends are not retired at all," says Vibrant Nation member Donna Hull. "They may have left their longtime jobs and occupations, but they've replaced them with hobbies, volunteer work, and new businesses. I don't know anyone who lounges around all day."

When the smart, successful women of VibrantNation.com talk about retirement, they often emphasize their interest in ongoing work — but in ways that are better aligned with their current values and priorities. For Donna, "retirement" simply meant shifting to self-employment. "Now that I work for myself, I don't think that I'll ever 'retire.' In fact, I'm finding that my travel- blogging business takes as much time as I can give it. I've turned into a workaholic, but one who's also seeking more balance in her life — and I'm loving every minute of it!"

Use your professional experience to serve your community in new and challenging ways. "After one year of marriage, I wondered why I was still teaching school, working 70-hour weeks, when I had a wonderful husband and stepson at home — so I retired," says Peg. She saw retirement as an opportunity to use her skills and experience to continue serving her community, but in a way that was freshly engaging and challenging. "My husband and I started a nonprofit to teach couples who are in financial distress both financial management skills and basic communication," she says. "I'm using my educational background to write the curriculum and am also learning how to build and maintain Web sites. I'm busy. I'm learning. And my husband and I are learning how to love each other and others. I couldn't be happier!"

Follow your passion. "My younger sister recently retired and has been attending art school," says Vibrant Nation member JC Eberhart. "Now she is selling her paintings. I've never seen her so happy!" Adds JC, "I'm 60 and I'm still on-staff full-time at a health center here in Minnesota. I love my work, but now I'm beginning to think about cutting back on work days to pursue my other passions: writing and art."

This is a path that Vibrant Nation blogger Sarah Carter

knows well. "The idea of painting was somewhere in the back of my mind, but I couldn't allow myself to take it seriously. I couldn't paint because I had always defined myself as a designer, not an artist. I wasn't allowed to paint — it wasn't who I was." Then, one day, when she was in her mid-50s, Sarah decided to buy some paintbrushes and oil paints and go to an art class. "I painted," says Sarah, "and I was just like a pig in mud. It's hard to put into words how right this felt. It was exactly what I wanted. I started to paint landscapes, and miraculously, people even wanted to buy them!"

Go back to school. Many boomer women put their professional dreams on hold for decades to focus on their families. "Retirement" for a generation of full-time wives and mothers can mean finally pursuing educational dreams long on the back burner. "My experience is all backwards," says Vibrant Nation blogger Sarah Swenson. "I worked professionally in educational administration and medical public relations in my 20s and early 30s. Then I stayed home to raise my children while doing professional volunteer work at an art museum as a gallery educator. But now my children are out of the house, my husband is history, and I'm back in school working on a graduate degree to become a counselor. I begin my internship at a big mental health center this week. I don't expect to bury myself the way I did in my 20s, working all hours of the day and night. I *do* expect to enjoy every minute, though, and I hope to be helpful to my clients for as long as I continue to feel capable and able to do so."

Remember, your husband's retirement is your retirement, too. If you're married, enjoying your retirement often involves helping your husband navigate his own transition. "Many men who've had long and successful careers need some help orienting to retirement," says Vibrant Nation member BKatz. "They may be stuck and need some prodding. Ask him: 'What are you passionate about? How can you feel useful in your family or community?'"

"Encourage him to find a new hobby," advises Anna Sue. "Find your own interests and have 'your time.' Go together to some activities and separately to others. Just because he is at home doesn't mean you have to be attached at the hip!"

"Do you live in the same location as when you were

working?" adds Vibrant Nation member and author Jan Cullinane. "One idea is to move to a master-planned community — tons of activities, new social contacts, a whole new world to explore. My husband and I moved to a new environment, and it is fabulous — he doesn't know where the day has gone."

Remember, this is your retirement, too. "I've seen too many women just continue on with all the 'womanly' chores while the man enjoys his retirement," says Marilynne. "When my husband started thinking about retirement, I told him I didn't want a husband I had to dust — I didn't want him sitting around in a chair all day. As a result, I have house cleaners come in and I get to eat out a lot. My husband and I take turns cooking. Neither of us is tied to the house; we're both happier."

Celebrate the empty nest by reclaiming your independent self. Vibrant Nation members know that the empty nest is more than merely an occasion to grieve. For women who have been full-time moms for 18 years or more, retiring from full-time motherhood is a wonderful opportunity to rediscover their independent selves.

"I surprised everyone when my daughter left for college two years ago," says Vibrant Nation member Melissa F. "We were very close and I had spent 18 years living my life for her, so everyone was afraid that I was going to be lost without her. What I didn't expect was that I would regain my old self after she left. I lost 40 pounds in five months, took on two part-time jobs on top of my full-time job, became the women's social director at my church, and rediscovered my relationship with my husband. I felt great! I felt younger, had more energy, and found that I didn't really miss my daughter so much after all. I still love to spend time with her, but I don't pine away for her. I'm enjoying my life as an independent adult. I enjoy having less responsibility and the ability to make last-minute plans and go out whenever I want to. And I love my new relationship with my young adult daughter."

8

Change the World

by Andrew Carle

Andrew Carle is an award-winning professor and founding director of the Program in Senior Housing Administration at George Mason University, Virginia, the first academic program in the nation dedicated exclusively to the field. He has received national and international recognition for defining a new category of senior housing, "University-based Retirement Communities" (UBRCs™), as well as a definition and categories for "Nana" Technology™ (technologies for older adults). Carle's work has been featured or cited in or on CNN, CBS News, NPR, the *New York Times*, *USA Today*, and *U.S. News & World Report*, among others, as well as numerous international media.

Today's new or soon-to-be retirees should be proud. As the leading edge of the "Baby Boom" (my own generation), you invented the personal computer, artificial heart, and rock and roll. You stood up for civil rights, women's rights, and disability rights. If the "Greatest Generation" saved the world (and they did), there can be little doubt you changed it.

But what if you were in a position to do the unthinkable? To change the world for the better not once . . . but twice?

By 2030 there will be more people over the age of 60 than under the age of 15 for the first time in our 300,000-year history as a species on the planet. We will literally be living in a different world than has ever been known before.

Unfortunately, society has done little to adjust to this new world. We live in suburban communities designed for families and cars. Our grown children have moved away, making the assistance they have traditionally provided difficult to receive. We have built senior housing communities that are a better alternative to nursing homes, yet the elderly are still often separated from the rest of society.

For boomer retirees, there are only two options. We can "get out of the way" and hope someone else takes care of these problems. Or we can try and fix them ourselves.

Betting that the generation that marched on

Washington will not settle for going quietly into the night, I offer two areas where we can use retirement to improve the quality not only of our adult lives, but also of every generation to follow.

Meet George Jetson

Technologies, including those targeted specifically to older populations, have made the lives of nearly everyone easier. One recent technology places sensors around the home, tracks movements, and reports unusual patterns of those living alone to a designated family member or friend. We've also seen automated medication dispensers that ensure distribution of the right dose at the right time, as well as safety devices that can recognize a fall and signal for assistance.

But such technologies are limited in function, and often constrain activities outside the home. Instead of sensors in the walls, why not in our clothes? Researchers are developing "iTextiles," clothing that can be washed and worn, and that will wirelessly monitor everything from blood pressure to heart rate, cholesterol, blood sugar, responses to medication, and falls. In a chapter from science fiction, scientists at MIT are working on a shirt that will incorporate nanotechnology (molecular engineering) to not only detect and report a heart attack, but physically contract and release to administer CPR.

Need help around the house? Japanese researchers are developing "assistance robots" that can see, hear, and smell, as well as empty the dishwasher, sweep the floor, and wash, dry, and fold laundry. "Rosie the Robot," only real.

Tired of losing the remote or getting up to turn off a light or change the thermostat? What if you could talk to your home? Voice recognition technology is advancing to allow virtually "human" conversation, including a refrigerator that will alert you when you are low on milk, even order it directly from the store.

Beyond the Commune

While such technologies hold promise, they will be meaningless if retirees are living in homes that don't additionally match their needs, preferences, and lifestyle.

An aging world will need "livable communities," places

that move houses from the back of the lot to the street, that make "walkable" the shopping and services people need. Places that provide housing for multiple generations on the same block, and parks where older adults can sit while children play.

It will also need better-designed homes. Homes either without stairs, or with bedroom and bath spaces on the ground floor. Such homes will have wider doors, better-lit hallways, zero-step entrances and showers, and kitchens with adjustable-height countertops, cabinets, and appliances. As we have learned from areas of public architecture, a "universal design" home would simply be a better home for people of all ages.

Finally, there will be a need for more choices in what retirees call "home."

Like to travel? How about retiring to a cruise ship? Enjoy wine? How about a community in Napa for wine connoisseurs? Belong to a niche culture or group? Retirement communities for groups from Asian Americans, to university alums, to lesbian, gay, bisexual, and transgender populations are beginning to enter the market. Through both their numbers and diversity, boomers have exploded the portfolio of products of every industry throughout their lives. Why settle for retirement and related senior housing communities that all look alike?

Talk About a Revolution

Totaling more than 70 million in the United States alone, boomers possess the critical mass, attitude, and experience in creating change to not only reinvent retirement, but eliminate ageism as the last "ism" of our time. If that weren't enough, we also possess something we did not have the first time around. We control 70 percent of the nation's wealth.

So here's suggesting we don't rest on our laurels. Instead, let's use our unique position to move advanced technologies out of the lab and into our daily lives by demanding that corporate America listen to our needs and purchasing power. Let's use our collective voices and political might to change zoning and construction regulations that currently place barriers on the creation of truly livable and intergenerational communities. To paraphrase the first president we elected to office, ask not what your retirement can do for you, but what you, as a generation, can do for retirement.

Thought 1969 was fun? By 2029 we can change the world — again.

9

A Cartoon

by Mort Gerberg

Mort Gerberg is a cartoonist and author best known for his magazine cartoons in numerous publications such as the *New Yorker*, *Playboy*, and *Publishers Weekly*.

He was voted Best Magazine Cartoonist of 2008 and 2007 by the international National Cartoonists Society. Gerberg also has drawn several syndicated newspaper comic strips and written, edited, and/or illustrated 40 books for adults and children.

Gerberg is the editor of *Last Laughs: Cartoons About Aging. Retirement . . . and the Great Beyond*, an original hardcover collection, and the author of *Cartooning: The Art and the Business*, the leading instructional/reference work in the field. Among his other popular books are the best-selling *More Spaghetti, I Say* and *Joy in Mudville: The Big Book of Baseball Humor*.

"Oh, you know with Leonardo, it's never retirement, it's always reinvention."

© Mort Gerberg 2007

Section

YOUR RETIREMENT GAME PLAN

10

What Happy Retirees Know

by Sydney Lagier

Sydney Lagier is a former certified public accountant. Since retiring from her finance career in 2008, she has been writing about the transition from productive member of society to "gal of leisure" on her blog, *Retirement: A Full-Time Job*. So far, she's learned that in retirement there are still not enough hours in a day, it's surprisingly hard to tell people at cocktail parties, what you "do" and having enough money is only one ingredient to a comfortable retirement. She and her also-retired husband live in Northern California.

T is a well-known fact that there are two categories of retirees (and by well-known fact, I mean that I am making it up here). In the first category, we have the folks who transition seamlessly into happy retirements. The second category tends to have a tougher time with this transition. This group may wonder whether they are really cut out for retirement at all.

You can find lots of advice out there about how to create a successful retirement, but most of the experts dispensing this advice share a common trait. They are usually financial planners, stockbrokers, tax advisors, or insurance agents, but it is not their financial acumen to which I refer. What they have in common is the fact that the vast majority of people doling out retirement advice are not yet retired. This means they are focused on one retirement concern, and one concern only: money.

I've been retired for nearly four years now. Hundreds of retirees have shared their stories with me. Having enough money is certainly a major concern for retirees, just as it is for nonretirees. But when that newly minted retiree wakes up on her first morning of retirement, it's not money she's thinking about. She's wondering what on earth she is going to do with the rest of her life.

She may be excited to return to some old hobbies she hasn't had time for over the years. Maybe she's got a stack of books that she can't wait to immerse herself in. Piano lessons, art classes, and travel destinations beckon. A growing list of unfinished projects around the house nags. And what about doing volunteer work or an exercise routine, or joining a book club?

My advice? Slow down. You've spent the last several decades being who your employer needed you to be. Now it's time to find out who you are without work. Don't overcommit yourself before you even get a chance to see who that is. What are the real secrets to creating a happy retirement? Ask the happy retirees.

Happy retirees are healthy. Enjoying good health was the single most important factor impacting retiree happiness, according to a 2009 Watson Wyatt analysis. Retirees in poor health were nearly twice as likely as their healthy peers to report being unhappy in retirement, trumping all other factors, including money and age.

Happy retirees have a significant other. The same study found that married or cohabiting couples are more likely than singles to be happy in retirement, and the news gets even better for couples enjoying retirement together. Retirees whose partners were also retired reported being happier than those with a working partner, according to research conducted at the University of Greenwich.

Happy retirees are social butterflies. The Greenwich study also found that having friends was far more important to retirement bliss than having kids. Those who had strong social networks were 30 percent happier with their lives than those without a strong network of friends. Surprisingly, having kids or grandkids had no impact on a retiree's level of contentment.

Happy retirees are not addicted to television. After you retire, you will have lots of time to fill. If you want to be happy in retirement, don't fill that time with endless hours of television. Frequent TV viewers report lower satisfaction with their lives, according to a 2005 study by the Institute for Empirical Research in Economics in Zurich. The same results were found again in 2008 by researchers at the University of Maryland. In that study, a direct negative correlation was found between the quantity of TV viewing and happiness levels; unhappy people watched more, happy people watched less.

Happy retirees are intellectually curious. Adults over 70 who chose to spend their time watching TV were two-and-a-half times more likely to suffer the effects of Alzheimer's than those who chose brain-stimulating activities instead, according to Richard Stim and Ralph

Warner's book, *Retire Happy: What You Can Do Now to Guarantee a Great Retirement*. Not only will shunning TV make you happier, it will make you healthier, which will, in turn, make you happier — a not-so-vicious cycle.

Happy retirees aren't addicted to achievement. The more that you are defined by your job, the harder it will be to adjust to life without it. According to Robert Delamontagne's book *The Retiring Mind: How to Make the Psychological Transition to Retirement*, achievement addicts have the most difficulty transitioning to retirement.

Happy retirees have enough money. Of course, you'll need enough money to support your chosen lifestyle in retirement, but most studies show that beyond that, more will not make you happier. The Watson Wyatt survey found that the precise amount of money you have for retirement is less important than how your retirement income compares to your income before retirement. If you have enough to continue your pre-retirement lifestyle, you have enough to be happy.

Happy retirees engage in volunteer or paid work. Researchers at the University of Maryland found that people who picked up a little work in retirement were healthier. And the benefits don't depend on how many hours you work; even temporary work had the same positive effects on health. Furthermore, you don't have to get paid to enjoy the benefits. A growing body of research shows that retirees who volunteer reap the same positive effects on health, happiness, and longevity as those who work for money.

There will be plenty of time to get into your retirement groove. Let it evolve naturally. Be open to where it leads you. Now is the time to discover who you are without work. You've earned this. Retirement is not a destination, it's a journey, so be sure to enjoy the detours.

II

65 and Lucky

by Bill Roiter, Ed.D.

Bill Roiter, Ed.D., is a psychologist, executive coach, businessman, author, and consultant to people as they move beyond work. Roiter's recent book, *Beyond Work: How Accomplished People Retire Successfully*, won the bookstore owners' and librarians' Axiom Gold Medal as the best retirement book of 2009. This essay is based on his research for the book. Also, Roiter is a clinical instructor at Harvard Medical School and a consultant to the Duke University Center for Genomic Medicine.

T here are two types of luck: one is random and one is made. Enjoy your life by making your luck work for you.

When I first talk to people about luck, they inevitably bring up winning the lottery — something that's clearly based on luck and on buying a ticket. If you don't buy a ticket, your chances of wining are reduced from some astronomical number to zero. This luck is based on the randomness of chance and is different from the luck I am talking about.

By age 65 you've had your share of luck, both good and bad. Now is the time to think about how you can increase your good luck and reduce your bad luck. It begins by understanding that what I'm writing about has little to do with chance and everything to do with preparation and opportunity. Consider those lucky people who bought Ford stock in 2009 when it was $1.94 and sold it when it hit almost $19.00. Any of us can buy a lottery ticket, but few of us know enough to buy a stock that in a year increases by $17.06 for every dollar invested. Those lucky bastards!

Jacques Cousteau said, "We must believe in luck. For how else can we explain the success of those we don't like?" Harsh, but it does ring true. It was Louis Pasteur who got to the heart of the type of luck I am writing about when he observed, "Chance favors the prepared mind." Preparation increases your luck by increasing your ability to see opportunities that you and others may miss; simply, you will see more opportunities when you prepare yourself to see them. The more opportunities you see, the greater are your chances of making them work for you. In basketball, you are more likely to shoot a basket if you have five opportunities to shoot rather than only one.

Preparation not only increases your ability to see opportunities; it also increases the likelihood of taking full advantage of them. When you have more shots at the basket, you become a better shooter because you learn from your mistakes; it's called practice. Here is an example: a retired schoolteacher I know had always wanted to be a tour guide in her native city. While having good knowledge of the city and a friendly personality, she had no experience or contacts in the tourism business. She decided to look for opportunities in the trade while learning more about it (*opportunity and preparation*). She mentioned to friends that she was seeking interesting work as a tour guide, and she began looking through classified ads. A friend's friend did some part-time work as a cruise ship "greeter" and told her about a blog that had local job postings. Cruise ships, docked in her town for a day, hired people from the area to greet passengers as they disembarked and to talk with them about the city. She answered the ad and was hired to greet the next ship. She eventually greeted eight more ships during the season. Soon after being hired, she had lunch with some of her fellow greeters, who told her about other opportunities for part-time tourism work. She now has more offers than she can handle and is having great fun. She considers herself quite lucky.

What would you like to be doing? Focus on one or two areas you would like to try and then prepare yourself by reading, listening, telling friends of your interest, and searching out opportunities. Find some people who are doing what you want to do, and ask them how they got involved with it. Speaking with others is a good way to scare up opportunities, but I find some people are reluctant to do this, for fear of looking foolish. If you feel that you might embarrass yourself, you can soften the conversation by saying to the other person that you are curious about how he or she started a new career, became a golf starter, got a job in a hardware or clothing store, or became involved in local government. A number of retired fishermen spend time at our town's fishing pier talking with visiting tourists. I've found that most people like to be asked about themselves and feel good about helping out someone else.

This is a time of life marked by changes that challenge us to think differently than we have before. Many people hope to reduce the uncertainty of this time by seeking certainty. It has been my experience that certainty is an illusion, while confidence is a possibility. Look to build your confidence in your ability; it will help you live well now and into the future. To do this, it is important to recognize that our priorities over the last 40 or so adult years were pinned to building a career, raising a family, and/or making a good life for ourselves. Those priorities change as we grow into our 60s, to be replaced by initial uncertainty and some confusion — "Now what do I do?" many of us ask. If you understand retirement as only "not working," you are left with little idea of what to do. I have learned that this time of life is built upon four areas of opportunities and challenges that structure our lives — our *financial, physical, social,* and *personal well-being.*

Learn about these areas, ask questions, gather information, consider what is important to you, experiment, and use your luck as you enjoy this exciting next chapter of your life. That should keep you busy for years to come.

12

Trump Fear with Purpose

Mary Lloyd is the author of *Supercharged Retirement: Ditch the Rocking Chair, Trash the Remote, and Do What You Love*. Her company, Mining Silver LLC, offers resources to help people create their own uniquely satisfying retirement. Lloyd started her career as a mining geologist when miners still objected to having women underground. She retired at age 47 as an executive-level manager in the natural gas industry to write novels, only to discover that the biggest challenge of retirement was finding any kind of challenge at all. After 13 years of struggling with that, she realized her "real work" is helping people focus better to get retirement right.

Once you retire, it's easy to start worrying. You might outlive your money. (That's a biggie.) You might lose your mental acuity. (Another biggie.) You might spend your last years alone. (Maybe these are *all* biggies…) But being afraid is a lousy way to live. It's also a first-class ticket to the very places you don't want to go — financial stress, poor health, and loneliness.

What should you do instead? Find something to be passionate about. Yep. A sense of purpose — and the work you do because of it — can make retirement much less fearful. That sounds like the exact opposite of the "golden years" experience we've been looking forward to. Not really. You don't need to spend every waking moment slaving away for some cause. But to keep your later years vibrant and satisfying, you *do* need something more important to think about than what you're going to have for dinner.

Why "purpose?" To really thrive, act on something more than your own needs. Taking action is the opposite of being a victim — and fear is a victim mindset.

Purpose helps you physically. In one study, nuns who reached advanced age never exhibited symptoms of Alzheimer's even though the physiological characteristics were evident when their brains were studied after they died. Why? In a religious order, they had work to do, even at age 100. Their lives went beyond themselves.

Purpose helps you emotionally. Focusing your effort on something you believe in confirms you're competent and relevant — reinforcement that's hard to find in a leisure-centered retirement. When you have high self-esteem, fear is less of an issue.

Purpose helps you mentally. Purpose stretches your mind. You learn new concepts so you can act on that purpose. You find solutions to further the cause. Acting on what's important keeps you alert and your world expanding.

Purpose helps you socially. Being involved in something bigger than walking the dog connects you to life on a much larger basis. You build new relationships because of your interest. You make contacts to learn more. Purpose will get you out of the house and involved while fear makes you shrink into a smaller and smaller version of life.

It's okay if you're already retired and now realizing you need more than a game of Mexican Train. You can find a purpose at any point in life. And you don't have to keep the same one forever. A good example of this is caring for an ailing parent. Once that loved one no longer needs your care, you'll want to find another purpose — at least if you're smart.

This is not a call to become the next Mother Teresa.

It doesn't have to be "save the world" stuff to be legitimate as a purpose. It doesn't need to be full-time. It just needs to be important — to *you*.

If You're Clueless...

If you have no idea what your purpose is or should be, you're definitely not alone. For most of our adult lives, the job served as our "purpose." That work may have been consistent with our values, or it may not have been. Regardless, we knew we had a purpose because we were "getting the job done." The paycheck proved it. After we retire, it's up to us to find a reason to keep on breathing.

But how do we do that? For some of us, there's been a little flame burning for years that just needs to be fanned. So if you have an inkling, be grateful and go for it. If your "retirement purpose" isn't already burning brightly, don't panic. There's a simple way to get started. To create a "starter purpose," look at two things:

- What do you believe strongly?
- What are you good at?

What Do You Value?

Take a sincere, quiet look at what you feel is important.

Not just for you, but for the larger good — the world, society, or your community. Maybe it's teaching kids personal responsibility. Maybe it's lobbying for more access to public lands for recreational hunting. There's *something* that either gets your ire up or makes you totally jazzed when you think about it.

To get at this information, start with what you like, what you don't like, or what your ideal world would include that the real one doesn't. You may have to dig through some layers of garbage or trivial matters to get to it, but when you find it, you'll know. You will feel yourself getting excited — and ready to take action.

What Do You Do Well?

The second piece of the equation involves awareness of what you're good at. It will be easy (or at least easier) to point to the skills and knowledge you gained from the work you did. But that's not the only place to look. You may have learned to be an incredible party planner while working 9 to 5 as an accountant. And don't just stop with what *you* think you're good at. Get feedback from family and friends.

This is about finding something to get involved in that makes you want to get up in the morning. Getting paid to do work you love doesn't hurt, but that's not the only reason to find a sense of purpose. Life is just plain better when you focus on more than your personal comfort.

A sense of purpose is the *first* thing anyone planning retirement needs to come up with — even before the money part. (Financial planning is easier if you know what you want to do, too.) Purpose helps you thrive. You stay involved in a community of like-minded others so you're not lonely. You use your mind, which keeps it healthy. You spend less on health care. (In fact, you don't notice the aches and pains as much when you're doing something you care about.) You'll have too much going on to spend time being afraid.

13

There's More to Retirement Planning Than Finances

Mike Bonacorsi is a CERTIFIED FINANCIAL PLANNER™

Mike Bonacorsi is a CERTIFIED FINANCIAL PLANNER™ and a professional speaker, author, and radio show host working with the baby boomer generation to help them become "retirement ready." His book *Retirement Readiness* has received awards from Reader's Reviews, the New England Book Festival, and Axiom Business Books. A 20-year veteran of the financial services industry, he serves on the board of the Financial Planning Association of Northern New England as pro-bono director and will serve as president in 2012. He is a member of the Life Planning Association (Boston) and the National Speakers Association and will serve as treasurer for the New England chapter beginning in May 2012.

The party last night was great! People you worked with 10, 15, even 20 years ago were there to wish you well. Even the head man from the regional office showed up. The stories about your career, the good and the bad times, went on all night. The new watch looked great on your wrist and the framed picture of the old crew will have a permanent place on the mantel. Yep, after 30 years at the company it was time to retire, but . . . retire to what?

Three months later, you're having an early cup of coffee wondering what the day will bring. The big trip you and your spouse had been anticipating has come and gone, the few projects around the house are near completion. You're fighting the urge to turn on the TV, with its ability to glue you to your chair for hours at a time. The daily chores have become just that — chores — and you're bored already. Is this really what you thought retirement would be?

Most people think of retirement planning as a financial process, but it should go beyond that. With life expectancies extending 20, even 30-plus years past traditional retirement, defining and planning how you want to spend your time in your later years is just as important as how you spend your money.

So, how will you spend your time? Do you have a plan for your time or will you awaken each morning and wing it from there? Think about it — this is what you have been looking forward to, the opportunity to plan your time and truly make it yours! Throughout your working years, your career owned your time 9 to 5, five days a week; what precious few hours remained had to be divided up amongst time with your family, running the household, friends, and activities. There just wasn't enough time to do all you wanted to do.

Now you have an open calendar, the opportunity to do what you want, and a chance to catch up on all you've wanted to do, but where do you start? To improve your chances for a successful retirement, I suggest you build your "lifestyle plan" the same way you would your financial plan.

Put your plan in writing — the commitment you make to a written plan is much stronger than you would make to a thought.

Be prepared to change, tweak, and adjust your plan as time goes on. Life is not a straight line, and a plan is never written in stone.

Share and discuss your plans with the person you will spend your retirement with, and listen to whatever plans he or she shares with you.

Begin with a list that contains all you want to

accomplish. The list should be more than "clean the cellar" or "go on vacation." It should include the specifics of your goals, what you want to accomplish, when you want to accomplish it, and why you want to accomplish it. The more real it becomes, the more you'll want to complete it. Consider the resources needed to accomplish each goal and how you will deal with any obstacles that might hinder your success.

Once the goals have been established and laid out, the next step is to plan your daily activities. You have 24 hours in a day and 365 days in a year — how are you going to use them? When you think about it, do we give time the respect it deserves? (It has more value than you might realize.) Once it passes, it cannot be recovered; a gold bracelet that is lost or gets sold can be replaced, but once time is gone, it's gone forever. We need to use every hour as best we can.

As you think about your day-to-day activities, consider what you want to do each week or month. Some of your activities will drive you to accomplish your goals. If you want to write the great novel, you might schedule an hour each day to work on it. If one of your goals is to lose weight and lower your blood pressure, you could set aside time each week for exercise. If you aren't 100 percent ready to walk away from the challenges of work or if you aren't as financially comfortable as you want to be, then scheduling a portion of your week to work has to be built into your plan.

As I work with clients, I suggest creating an ideal month. A month seems to be a good time frame to cover activities that occur less frequently than on a daily or weekly basis. Again, start with a list of what you want to do and how often you want to do it. If you are a writer who has set aside an hour each day to write, then you might want to include time to exercise on Mondays, Wednesdays, and Fridays. Time with your friends and family, time for chores, and time for yourself (quiet time with no one around) should all be part of your plan.

Planning your time is not new to you, but in the past you may not have had the luxury of creating your schedule around your wants or needs; now you can.

Once you have a plan in writing (rule 1) and you are prepared to make adjustments when necessary (rule 2), the next step is rule 3: to share and discuss your plans with the person you will spend your retirement with and to listen to whatever plans he or she shares with you.

Most of us have someone we plan on spending the next stage of life with — a spouse, partner, or companion. It's important for you to realize that that person also has goals and dreams to work toward, and you need to put time in your plan to help him or her succeed at achieving theirs.

So, it's the morning after your retirement party. Have you planned for your time as well as you've planned your finances? Remember, the success of your retirement depends on more than how much your 401(k) is worth!

Mike Bonacorsi LLC is a registered investment adviser. Securities offered through LPL Financial. Member FINRA/SIPC.

14

Retirement Is an Opportunity to Rethink Your Life and Do Something Different

by Susan Kersley

Susan Kersley was a doctor who wanted to be more creative and experience a different life. She studied personal development and had extensive counseling training (including earning a master's degree) while still working as a doctor. She was introduced to coaching by reading the books of Louise Hay and Thomas Leonard and then trained as a coach. She wrote a series of articles in the *British Medical Journal* about coaching in relation to the lives of doctors, and she has published several books for doctors and people about to retire. Now she paints, writes, coaches, and enjoys life. Her Web sites are www.getreadyforretirement.co.uk, www.thedoctorscoach.co.uk, and www.lifeaftermedicine.co.uk.

P erhaps you are approaching retirement and wondering what it will be like not to go to work anymore. If so, then I offer you some hints and tips about how to approach retirement and the opportunities it can bring you.

When you reflect on work, you may be referring to working for an employer, and you may be wondering what life will be like when you are no longer doing something that you've been involved in for many years. A number of people do continue working after retirement, though the type of work may be very different from their previous employment. For example, they may decide to set up their own business, do some volunteer work, or pursue whatever it is that they really feel drawn to doing.

If the thought of losing your daily work routine worries you, and you wonder how you will pass your days without it, then take heart and be reassured that new opportunities will open up for you when you retire. What these are may depend to some extent on what you really would like to do after you retire.

Some people are very anxious about lack of income, and they might want to find suitable paid employment. Remember that this could be something entirely different from your previous job. Perhaps there is something you love doing as a hobby, and now you could find a way to be financially compensated for it. The rate of pay might be less than before, but nevertheless it is still something that would occupy your days and also bring you a bit of extra income.

If, on the other hand, you have adequate retirement funds, you may be able to volunteer to help in any number of worthy organizations, and perhaps to raise funds for a charity you support. There is a wealth of other activities you can consider doing as well, including writing your life story, playing golf, learning another language, traveling around the world, or anything you wished you had time for when you were working.

As with everything, the most important question to ask yourself is, "What do I want?" Then make sure you answer yourself in great detail, so that you are able to identify something suitable that you'd like to spend your time doing.

Whatever you decide to do, avoid putting yourself into a stressful situation. It's very important at this stage of your life to be able to enjoy yourself, in addition to finding plenty to do each day.

If you have enough money from your pension, other retirement fund, or savings, then you might be able to learn new skills or indulge your passion for something you didn't have time for previously.

A common experience of retired people is that as time goes by, they discover many things they hadn't realized were available to them, and their days fill up quickly, so much so that they say, "I'm so busy now, I don't know how I ever had the time to work!"

You can find new things to do and to explore, things you've been putting off for years. Recognize that you can make up for lost time and get on with what you want to do. However, it's also important not to neglect your own health and well-being. Here are some things to do every day:

Get Fit, and Exercise Daily

As you get older, you may become more prone to illnesses, and find that you begin to deteriorate physically and mentally, too. To delay those changes as long as you can, it's important to look after yourself and to make up for years when there may have been a lack of self-care when you were working.

Keeping your body moving and your muscles and joints in good condition are vital for remaining fit and well for as long as you can. Exercise also helps to speed recovery if you become ill. The best sort of exercise as you get older is walking. If you take a walk most days for about half an hour, you will keep your heart beating well and your metabolism at a good rate, too. In addition to walking, you could practice yoga, which is useful because it helps you to relax and also enables your joints and muscles to remain functioning well. They say that yoga affects your mind, too, and that a flexible body is related to a flexible mind.

Eat Properly

Don't fall into the trap of living on bread and jam. Eat plenty of healthy foods. If you don't enjoy cooking, there are senior centers that offer activities and a hot meal. It's not difficult to eat simple things that are both healthy and inexpensive. For example, baked beans on toast, or baked potato and grated cheese with salad are healthy and will fill you up, and they are better for you than junk food. Make sure you eat plenty of vegetables and fruit every day, too.

Keep Your Mind Active

You can spend time reading all those books you never had the time for in the past, or you can enroll in a class or two to get up to speed with computers and the Internet, or you can join a club that meets socially and has regular informative talks.

Keep in Touch with Friends and Family

Make regular connections with your friends, both those you have now and perhaps some from the past whom you have lost touch with. And don't forget family. Make sure you speak on the telephone and visit as often as you can.

By doing these things, you'll be able to discover a whole world of opportunities to enjoy during your retirement. Remember, retirement is not about doors closing — it's more about the opening of a myriad of new opportunities and possibilities to enjoy.

15

Live to 100!

by Dr. Thomas T. Perls

Dr. Thomas T. Perls completed his training in internal medicine at Harbor-UCLA Medical Center in Torrance, California, and in geriatrics at Harvard Medical School and Mount Royal Hospital in Melbourne, Australia. The founder and director of the NIH-funded New England Centenarian Study, the largest study of centenarians and their families in the world, Perls is the coauthor of the award-winning book *Living to* 100, *Lessons in Maximizing Your Potential at Any Age.*

I 've studied centenarians now for more than 12 years. These are people, mind you, who have lived at least 40 years beyond the age of 60. A current centenarian was 60 years old in 1970. Whoever thought that when people turned 60 they might still have the equivalent of a whole other adulthood ahead of them! But now, centenarians are the fastest-growing segment of our population, and we so frequently hear about them that they raise the bar for the rest of us in terms of what life expectancies we see for ourselves.

What life expectancy should we expect? The Seventh Day Adventist Health Study reveals that most of us should be able to live to our mid-to-late 80s. Following the rules of their religion, Seventh Day Adventists are vegetarian and regularly exercise, don't smoke, and don't drink alcohol. (Though, perhaps drinking a bit of alcohol every day is good for you.) In addition, their weekends are dedicated to their faith and family. Perhaps the emphasis upon faith and family allows these people to effectively manage their stress. The result of these behaviors is that the Adventists have the longest average life expectancy in the world — approximately 88 years.

Unlike the Adventists, however, average life expectancy for most people in industrialized nations is currently 77 years or 10 years less. The reasons are not difficult to guess. Over 70 percent of Americans are overweight; 30 percent of these are obese; people still smoke cigarettes; only 15 percent of people regularly exercise; and diets that promote obesity, heart attacks, strokes, diabetes, and cancer are prevalent. As a Scandinavian twins' study points out, the vast majority of how old people can live is determined by their health-related behaviors. What's more, the New England Centenarian

Study noted that close to 90 percent of centenarians were independently functioning at the average age of 92 years — compressing the time that they aren't well toward the end of their exceptionally long lives. The centenarians thus show us that it is not a matter of "the older you get, the sicker you get," but rather, "the older you get, the healthier you've been." This empowering and optimistic view very likely applies to anyone who can come close to achieving the lifespan his/her body and environment are built for. No longer should we assume that life after 60 is a downhill slide. Instead, most people should be able to live nearly 30 additional years, most of that time independently. Good health habits are the prerequisite.

So what are the good health habits or characteristics that help people maximize their life expectancy and the time that they are healthy? The acronym AGEING (the British spelling of aging) will help you remember some of the most important points:

Attitude. Centenarians tend to be funny, gregarious, and optimistic. They manage their stress, shedding it instead of internalizing it. Thus, attempt to acquire a centenarian attitude.

Genetics. While you can't change your genes, you certainly can learn from them. Assess the longevity in your family. Do your relatives generally die in their 90s and older? Or do they die in their 60s or 70s? If the former, that is wonderful news for you. Longevity runs very strongly in families. Perhaps you can even indulge a bit in not-so-healthy habits — but only once in a while! On the other hand, if your relatives generally die in their 60s and 70s, alarm bells should be going off. It is very important that you participate in a diligent program of prevention and screening so that you either prevent or catch problems before they catch you.

Exercise. Exercise 30 minutes a day, at least five days a week. And, as you get older, weight lifting (strength training) becomes all the more important to regain and prevent muscle loss. Muscle doesn't just keep you strong and help with your balance and prevent falls. Increasing your muscle mass prevents osteoporosis (bone loss and fractures), improves sleep, burns fat, and can even help your memory. You can build muscle at any age.

Interests. Just as it is important to exercise your different muscles, it is also important to exercise different parts of your brain. To do this, take on new cognitive activities that you haven't performed before. For example, bridge, Scrabble, or Sudoku. The most powerful activities are learning a new language or musical instrument. Once you become good at the activity, move on to something new and difficult. Exercising your brain, at any age, can delay the onset or progression of memory loss and other cognitive problems that can be associated with aging.

Nutrition. The most important point about nutrition is to be on a diet that helps you maintain a healthy weight. Obesity is strongly associated with most age-related diseases. It is wise to stay away from sweets, minimize red meat in your diet, and keep an eye on your total number of calories per day.

Get rid of smoking and quackery. Smoking is without a doubt the worst possible thing most people can do to their bodies, and except in the case of a few rare individuals, it inevitably leads to lung and vascular disease. For many people it leads to various types of cancer. In my life expectancy calculator, smoking takes 15 years off your life. Also, antiaging quackery will certainly take money out of your wallet and lead to no benefits. In the case of some aggressively promoted treatments, such as growth hormone, there is the real possibility that the purported fountain of youth could contribute to your dying sooner and your suffering from numerous adverse effects of the drug.

Many people reading this book are, of course, 60 years old or older. As such, with a well-functioning brain, you are already demonstrating significant survival prowess. My guess is that you have a better chance than the average population of going even beyond the mid-to-late 80s! It is never too late to begin the strategies I have mentioned here. Those with friends and family younger than them should pass on this information, because one can't be too young to institute these healthy behaviors.

Well, now that you have another 30 or more years ahead of you, you know that you will be able to do the other 64 things mentioned in this book while looking forward to "Seventy-Five Things to Do When You Retire."

Other Resources

www.livingto100.com (a life expectancy calculator with feedback for what you are doing right and wrong and some guidance)

www.bumc.bu.edu/centenarian (the New England Centenarian Study Web site)

16

Positive Aging — Old Is the New Young

by Dave Bernard

Dave Bernard is not yet retired but has begun his due diligence to plan for a satisfying retirement. With a focus on the nonfinancial aspects of retiring, he is a weekly contributor to the U.S. *News & World Report* "On Retirement" blog and shares his discoveries and insights on his personal blog, *Retirement — Only the Beginning.*

S ay it isn't so. Out walking this morning, I glanced down at my short-pant-clad legs and saw something I had not noticed before. The last time I looked at my legs, I remember seeing nicely toned, could-be-a-little-more-tanned thighs holding me up. Today, I swear I saw the legs of an "older" man. Nothing drastic but you know how the skin seems to have been overstretched just a bit and is not clinging as tightly to the muscles beneath? Then it dawned on me — I am getting older, not just on the inside but on the outside as well.

How was it possible for aging to catch up with me? I have been an exercise fanatic since college and even today have a regular routine. I ride the stationary bike three to four times a week, lift weights twice a week, and do yoga twice a week. On the weekends, my wife and I take a long walk in the nearby hills or on the beach. We eat very well (avoiding fat and salt), go organic whenever we can, and do not overeat. Sure, we are both over 50 now, but what the heck! I guess when it comes to aging, you can run but you cannot hide.

Fortunately, I have always been a realist. I accept the facts for what they are and go with the flow. This aging thing is just another part of my life, and I need to realize and accept that fact. Aside from the physical aspects (I will miss my young legs), I realize there are many positives that have come with my advancing years and varied experiences:

1. **Appreciate your accomplishments.** I have successfully raised two wonderful children who make me proud each time we interact. Each has grown into a young adult filled with those values that are important in life

and critical to their continuing happiness. Had I not grown "older" (not old), I would not have been with them each step of the way, helping where needed, encouraging on occasion, and admiring their progress often. I would not change any of it for the world.

2. **Never stop learning.** Friends and family may quickly point out that I have a ways to go, but I have been learning along the way. I know not to sweat the little things but instead to accept that not everything will go the way I want, nor necessarily should it. I have learned the immeasurable value of my family, who have been with me through numerous difficult times, supporting and loving me. Without them, I would not be the person I am today (or maybe even here today). I realize that it is okay to cry, because if you feel like crying, there is a reason. I have learned that my wife is my best friend, my confidant, consciously blind to my faults, always there when I need her. I have learned that money does not make the moment nor buy happiness — that can only be found within you. Wisdom truly does come with age to the extent that we have experienced the ups and downs of many years lived, learned from those experiences, and incorporated that knowledge into our daily lives. It

did not kill us, so it must have made us stronger!

3. **Find your passion**. Pursuing a passion is what ultimately makes each day worth living. I realize that I have worked 30 years at various jobs to make a living. Although a worthwhile, noble pursuit, earning a living is not always inspirational, and it is often the exception rather than the rule that I arise with the excitement, energy, and urge to get to it. I am not complaining — I did what I had to do, met some wonderful people along the way, participated in the growth of multiple companies, and survived. But my advice to those starting down the employment path or still early in their careers is to find your passion. It is far better to start your day wanting to get going, anxious to do what you love, and be a force to be dealt with. Things don't always work out exactly the way you planned the first time, or even the second, but being passionate about what you are doing can in itself drive a stubborn refusal to quit. If you do what you love, the money will follow. And even if it is not a fortune, don't trade your happiness for the promise of a big bank account. In retired life, as in the working world, it is important to have passions to pursue each day to give you a reason to get out of bed and expectantly face the new day.

4. **Live today.** I cannot change the past, I do not know what the future holds, so my best bet is to live in this present moment. My aim is to focus on today, now, and live it fully. It is up to me to actively participate in and enjoy my retirement life, *now*. Tomorrow is never guaranteed, so don't wait.

> *As we advance in life it becomes more and more difficult, but in fighting the difficulties the inmost strength of the heart is developed.* — Vincent van Gogh

Life is a journey, and our faithful travel companion through it all is our aging mind and body. We can attempt to prepare for the trip with maps and well-laid plans and hopeful wishes, but the road ultimately leads where it will. The best way to enjoy the trip is to appreciate each moment, each new sight and sound and feeling. Live, learn, love, and keep going. Who knows what lies beyond the next sunrise?

Expand Your Social Circle — Face to Face

by Susan RoAne

Susan RoAne, aka The Mingling Maven® because of her classic book, *How to Work a Room*®, is one of the leading experts on savvy business networking. She is also a speaker who has shared her communication strategies with corporate and convention audiences as well as the new admirals and brigadier generals in our military. RoAne is known for her practical advice and for what Herb Caen, the late *San Francisco Chronicle* journalist, called "her dynamite sense of humor."

Incorporating social networking into our daily lives is a way to stay in touch with our family, friends, former colleagues, and networks. Being digitally connected is convenient, especially when we are retired. All we have to do is turn on our computers and log onto Facebook, e-mail, favorite blogs, chat rooms, or newspapers.

Online connections are seductive because we feel we are really "in touch" with others. However, while valuable, digital communication does not replace the in-person social interaction so important for our overall mental and physical health.

The "Cold" Hard Facts

Results from a study at UCLA captured my attention. It stated that seniors who were socially active had fewer colds. While I'm sure that the term "seniors" refers to people in their 80s, I was intrigued because I thought that being around people and their germs would have had the opposite effect. The authors of the article attributed their finding to the fact that being around others not only prevents social isolation, it also builds up our immunity. Who knew?! "Immunity in the community" sounds like a good motto to me.

Involvement Is Invaluable

In retirement, we need to plan our social lives and our face-to-face activities. Rather than wait for the phone to ring or invitations to appear, we must be proactive and pick up the phone or send an e-mail invitation and be the "inviter."

In retirement, we have the opportunity to become more

involved in our community and to expand our social networks that may have narrowed over the years. This is the perfect time to reach out to family and friends and to meet new people — whether through hobbies, places of worship, charities, or volunteer work. Getting out of the house and interacting face to face with others can broaden your horizons and give you more to look forward to.

Don't Be "List-less"

Grab a pencil and pad (legal pad or iPad) and write the following three headings. Then write in your responses to each statement. When you're done, you may have a clearer sense of the kind of retirement you want to pursue.

List #1: **"If the world were perfect and money wasn't an object, I would do:"** This list allows for unlimited, free-range thinking. It's a bucket list of sorts. See how many items on your list involve sharing with other people.

List #2: **"What I like to do:"** Whether it's playing poker or bridge, quilting, playing Scrabble or golf, supporting favorite teams, coaching, cooking, gardening, or spending time with grandchildren, you'll find there's a wealth of things to do with others — face to face.

List #3: "What I know, do well, and can share with others:" After years of work at a vocation and often an avocation, we have expertise to share as a tutor or mentor. Or we can teach a course through a community college or local nonprofit. Nothing is more fulfilling than getting involved — whether as a student or a teacher!

Share Your Stories

Because we have worked at our craft or our profession and lived our lives, we not only have skills and experience, but we also have stories. Many of our stories are instructive, interesting, and amusing — and deserve to be shared.

You never know how your experience may inspire another person's life or help him or her through a difficult time. Another way to make a difference is to share your stories by speaking at organizations or schools. There are also local Toastmasters groups across the country that can help you hone your messages and presentation.

Widen Your Circle

If a group doesn't exist that you would like…*start one.* Invite five people. Have them each invite a friend.

Meet at a local coffee shop or gathering place. Ask people to bring their most amusing retirement story. That starts the group on a high note.

According to research originally done through the Stanford Shyness Clinic, about 90 percent of us self-identify as being shy. If that's true for you, the upside is you have a lot of company. Knowing that others are uncomfortable in the face-to-face space, we can rely on the good manners and social graces we boomers were taught and, at any gathering, extend a warm welcome. Just because you're retired doesn't mean you have to be "shy and retiring!" Taking the small risk of saying hello can yield a huge reward: you could meet a new tennis partner, book club crony, or poker pal and make a new friend.

18

Career Women and Retirement: 6 Important Tips

by Helen Dennis and Bernice Bratter

Helen Dennis, a nationally recognized leader on issues of aging, employment, and the new retirement, has received awards for her university teaching and contributions to the field of aging. Editor of two books, popular speaker, and author of over 40 articles, she has assisted over 10,000 employees to plan for the nonfinancial aspects of their retirement. Her weekly "Successful Aging" column for the *Daily Breeze* and six additional newspapers reach 1.3 million readers plus those online. She is coauthor with Bernice Bratter of the *Los Angeles Times* best seller, *Project Renewment, The First Retirement Model for Career Women*. Her expertise is sought by employers, national publications like the *Wall Street Journal*, and such network news programs as ABC's *Primetime*.

Bernice Bratter is a licensed Marriage and Family Therapist and has advocated for both women and the aging. She was the executive director of the Center for Healthy Aging, president of the Los Angeles Women's Foundation and served on the Board of Directors of a Fortune 500 health care corporation. Under her leadership the Center for Healthy Aging became viewed as a national model for disease prevention and health promotion services for older adults. In recognition of her work in the nonprofit world, she received numerous awards including an Honorary Doctor of Law degree from Pepperdine University and was featured on 60 Minutes, 20/20, and Hour Magazine. She is coauthor of Project Renewment: The First Retirement Model for Career Women. Now retired, she continues her interests in women's issues, writing, and ongoing education.

F or the first time in history, millions of highly effective career women are facing retirement. They are part of the Silent Generation born between 1935 and 1964, and the first wave of the Baby Boom generation born between 1946 and 1955. The women of these two generations have their own unique characteristics, yet they share one in common: the lack of a retirement model that reflects their work history, drive, desires, values, and aspirations.

In 1999 this need served as the impetus for us to launch Project Renewment®, a forum and process for highly effective women to channel their drive and passion in developing their next chapter in life to be equal to or even more fulfilling than their previous one.[1]

"Renewment" is a word we made up as an alternative to retirement. "It suggests rebirth, choices, vitality, opportunity and personal growth. It implies that decisions about the next chapter of life can be intentional rather than defined by the needs and expectations of others."[2]

We have learned a great deal from these extraordinary women over a period of 10 years.

Here are some highlights and tips:

1. **Identity.** "Who am I without my business card?"[3] Professional identity is one of the biggest losses in retirement, particularly for those who love or have loved their work. Here's an exercise. Describe yourself to a colleague or friend, avoiding any reference to your career or work role. Think about a new identity and language you might use.

2. **Keeping busy.** The early phases of retirement are filled with "catch-up" choices. It's a chance to catch up with friends, clean the garage, toss clothes not worn for five years, cook your favorite dishes, and read the morning newspaper in the morning — on paper or a screen. Yet as time passes, what is it that keeps us busy? An empty calendar may feel like a threat. Yet, keeping a busy schedule is not the same as being fulfilled. So experiment and take a deep breath.

3. **Passion.** Passion is a source of intense energy. It has motivated career women to master tasks, achieve goals, and share with others. It is the impetus for creativity. We each have the capacity to experience passion-driven purposes. A commonly expressed concern is, "Can I find passion in retirement?" Retired or "renewment women" have discovered new passion in writing, launching a nonprofit, learning, and spending time with friends and grandchildren. Try something new or return to a previous love. Transfer that positive intensity to what is important to you at this life stage.

4. **Exercise.** Dr. Walter Bortz, noted geriatrician at Stanford University, warns us of the importance to avoid frailty in older age. The prevention can start early. The National Institute on Aging recommends four types of exercises that will improve health and abilities and postpone physical frailty: (a) endurance exercises such as jogging, cycling, speed walking, and swimming; (b) strength exercises such as resistance training and Pilates; (c) balance exercises such as yoga and Pilates; and (d) flexibility exercises such as yoga, Pilates, or ballet.

5. **He retires first.** This happens. The timing of

retirement among couples can be complex. Men and women have different work histories and retirement timetables. Often, women have entered the labor force later, reaching the peak of their careers as their husbands are ready to retire. What is required is good communication between mates. Discuss your vision of retirement and your expectations from one another. Most important, be good to one another.

6. **Our looks.** Society and the workplace have sent us strong messages — looking "older" is not necessarily considered an asset. How we "manage" our looks is a personal decision. Today, we have a huge antiaging industry that includes foods, nutritional supplements, age-defying hair products, cosmetic surgery, and remedies for sexual dysfunction and memory improvement. The largest organization that fights aging is the American Academy of Anti-Aging Medicine, with a membership of 11,500 physicians, health practitioners, and scientists in 65 countries. Many researchers disagree that aging can be stopped or reversed. They agree that the most effective approach to slow aging is making good lifestyle decisions such as engaging in physical and mental activity; eating a healthy diet of complex carbohydrates, fruits, and vegetables; leading

a purposeful life; and having meaningful relationships.

Hopefully these tips will help you shape your next chapter of life — as the best chapter. And Happy Renewment from both of us.

[1] Project Renewment® is a movement that has grown virally. Over 25 Renewment groups of 10 to 12 women are meeting throughout the country. They use the book *Project Renewment: The First Retirement Model for Career Women*, a *Los Angeles Times* best seller, as their guide. The book consists of 38 essays on topics most frequently discussed and a guide on how to launch and sustain a Project Renewment group with topics, questions for discussion, and group process recommendations.

[2] Ibid., p. 2.

[3] Ibid., p. 37.

19

Women and Retirement: Inventory Your Successes

by Judy Juricek

Judy Juricek is the president of Attract Your Ideal Retirement, Inc. She is passionate about helping women in their 40s, 50s, and 60s plan for, attract, and live their ideal lives in retirement. Juricek has many years of private and public-sector Human Resources experience, holds a certification as a Senior Professional in Human Resources, and a master's of management in technical education. When she is not working, she enjoys spending time with her family at the beach or doing anything challenging for her body and mind.

Congratulations! You certainly deserve a hearty pat on the back. After all, you have successfully navigated a treacherous business world to reach your career pinnacle. At the same time, perhaps you were raising a family, helping your partner get ahead with his or her career, volunteering in the community, and assisting other family and friends who needed your help. You have truly done an amazing job reaching this point in your life.

Off the top of your head, can you name all of your successes since you entered adulthood? For most people, the answer is no. As you retire, please consider taking some time to sit down and inventory all of your successes and achievements, and compile them in a list. This will help you to see that, simply put, success builds upon itself; if you can create success once, you can replicate it again and again, even in different circumstances.

For example, at some point in your career, you worked hard to get a much-coveted promotion. You took on extra assignments (maybe even a new job title, with no additional pay but more responsibility), toiled a lot of extra hours, and proved your worthiness to the company. Even though you may not have formally sat down to document your accomplishment with that promotion, you likely remember that you were bursting with pride and confidence. In later attempts to tackle a new job or another promotion, you were much more likely to feel that you could succeed because you had done it before.

Here is another example of how success builds upon itself. Put yourself in the shoes of a small-business owner who has just made his or her first sale. If your product is appealing enough for a customer to spend hard-earned money on it, then most likely more people will recognize the product's value, buy it, and help you to replicate the first success (with proper marketing, of course).

Making a success inventory doesn't require money, but you will need an environment for quiet reflection. To start the process, take out a pad of paper or turn on your computer. You should list — from the beginning of your adult life to the present — all of the things that you have achieved (school, work, family, church, volunteering — the categories are endless). Be as specific as possible. Bear in mind that you don't have to do this all in one sitting. Take your time, and really step back and think about how you felt at the very moment you reached your goal. Remember, if you had success once, you can do it again.

When you take a final look at the long list, you will be amazed at your achievements. Then, pat yourself on the back (which is something we all need to do more often).

You can use this list in a variety of ways. It can be a springboard to think about what you want to accomplish in the next phase of your life — retirement. What skills are common threads running through your list? Looking forward, how can you build on these skills to craft your ideal life in retirement?

If you plan to continue working in some capacity, you can use the list to augment your résumé or curriculum vitae. If you want to continue in the same career field, it is important to list achievements that pertain to the job you are seeking. It's easy to overlook an important achievement, particularly when you have a lot of them, but you never know what an employer is looking for.

You can also use your achievement list to identify job opportunities in different fields. Perhaps you did some public speaking in the job that you are retiring from, and you want to do more. By identifying what you want to do next, you can pinpoint the existing skills that you need to develop.

Similarly, you can use the list to dust off an old dream that had been set aside long ago. Perhaps you wanted to be a sailor, or a model, or a dentist, or even a hot-air balloon operator. If you decide that you still want to pursue this dream, do you have the skills necessary, or will you need to build new ones? Will you need to bring your dream into today's world, and modify it for your current stage of life?

As you can see, making a list of your achievements is a powerful exercise that can be used in a variety of ways. At a minimum, it can help you transition from one facet of your life to another, and it can validate all of your hard work. At a maximum, it can help you craft your ideal life in retirement (you deserve that after working a lifetime, right?). The list should, at the very least, remind you of how awesome you really are — and that alone is an investment of time well spent.

20

Choices

by Elizabeth Doucet

Elizabeth Doucet has been practicing law for 40 years. She graduated from Temple University in Philadelphia, Pennsylvania, with a degree in journalism and from Loyola School of Law, New Orleans, Louisiana. Before attending law school, she was a reporter for United Press International in Philadelphia (1963) and South Vietnam (1965–66). She concentrates her practice on employment law and bankruptcy. She and her husband moved to Louisiana in 2005 to return to her first love — writing — two months before Hurricanes Katrina and Rita devastated parts of Louisiana and Mississippi. She volunteers at four local organizations and teaches family law and English at a private college in Lake Charles, Louisiana.

My middle initial is "H" but it should have been "R" for risk taker, which I have always been. For example, in my early 20s I traveled with my former husband to report on the war in South Vietnam. The possibility of getting killed never entered my mind. So, the idea of picking up and leaving the town in Ohio where we had lived for 20 years and moving 1800 miles away to a place where we knew no one was not a big deal to me. Someone said it better than me many years ago. Choice is everything.

For years, the idea of retiring frightened me. Money was the biggest issue, or for years it was the greatest deterrent to my actually retiring. A dear friend, who had retired earlier, encouraged me to retire, assuring me that "things just happen" to make it all work out. But because I had so much debt and a daughter to put through college, I kept pushing the idea of retirement further and further back. Then, one of my employees embezzled almost half a million dollars from my trust fund. After that, the snow in Ohio seemed to fall earlier and harder, and to accumulate in greater depths.

Thus, in January 2004 I looked at a map of the United States to see where we might move to. I had lived in New Orleans and its suburbs for 12 years and I still felt as though Louisiana was home. Although I was a Yankee, having been raised in Philadelphia, Pennsylvania, in my heart I knew I wanted to get back to writing instead of practicing law. Living in Louisiana made sense. I also knew that I needed a roof over my head. New

Orleans would have been the natural place to go (thank heavens I did not choose it), I knew that with so many of my friends still living there I would never complete my writing projects. We had visited Lake Charles, Louisiana, many years before. And, when I worked for the *Times-Picayune* I had been friends with the son of the publisher of the *American Press*, which was the Lake Charles daily, so I decided to check out Lake Charles on the Web. I wrote to its Tourist and Convention Bureau and soon after received a guide to the city, which contained a listing of local realtors, one of whom I contacted. Two weeks later I was on my way to Lake Charles.

I was quickly charmed by the town because the restroom signs were in French. Lake Charles is part of Acadiana was settled in the 1700s by the Acadians expelled from the Maritime Providences. Their influence is everywhere.

The first part of the weekend I toured homes. Pinnacle had not yet opened its large casino and resort L'auberge du lac, so home prices were considerably below the national average, as was the cost of living. As for the arts, there is a symphony (until recently conducted by Tony Kushner's father, William), a ballet company, a Reform Jewish congregation, and several Chinese restaurants. And, while I was visiting Lake Charles, the temperatures by noon were in the 70s while folks in Ohio were shivering in the teens. I felt silly carrying my sheared beaver coat. To top it off, I could get the Sunday *New York Times* delivered to my home.

That June my husband, a trailing spouse for many years, took his turn checking out Lake Charles. He returned with the same favorable impression I had had of the area. The people were great. The prices and cost of living were right.

Shortly thereafter I purchased a place in a suburb of Lake Charles, Moss Bluff. We sold our house in Ohio and our business and moved in June 2005. From the moment we drove onto our street in Moss Bluff, I knew I was home.

Choice is everything. The right choice can mean success, happiness, contentment, great friends, and an interesting and busy retirement. The wrong choice can become an expensive decision.

For example, one of my dearest friends chose to move from sunny California to a retirement community in Florida. Although the physical location of the community was appealing, she was never happy there. She and her family did not fit in with the community, the hurricanes were too much for her and her husband to deal with, and she missed her friends. After three years she returned to California, abandoning her Florida house to foreclosure as the housing market tanked.

It is almost six years since we chose Lake Charles. I am deeply involved in the community. I am president of one of three little theater groups in Lake Charles, on the board of two other organizations, and legal counsel to the master gardener group. Our family today includes three cats, a Border Collie, and a Moluccan Cockatoo. We have more friends and things to do than we ever had in Ohio. We have never looked back. Yes, choice is everything and I'm glad we made the right one. May you make choices that are right for you, too.

Budget for 100 Years

by Anna Rappaport, F.S.A., M.A.A.A.

Anna M. Rappaport, F.S.A., M.A.A.A., founded Anna Rappaport Consulting in 2005 after retiring from Mercer Human Resource Consulting. She chairs the Society of Actuaries Committee on Post-Retirement Needs and Risks, which is active in building solutions for a better retirement for Americans. Rappaport has worked on retirement issues within the American Academy of Actuaries and is on the boards of the National Academy of Social Insurance, the Pension Research Council, the Women's Institute for a Secure Retirement (WISER), and the Actuarial Foundation.

Whether already settled into your retirement or looking forward to it with anticipation, it's not too late to plan for the unexpected at age 60. Like many in the Golden Watch Generation, you've anticipated that this new stage of life will open up a whole new world of opportunities — for seeing family and friends, for travel, and for other leisure activities. But you could be fooling yourself. According to recent research conducted by the Society of Actuaries (www. soa.org), there are serious gaps between perceptions about retirement and reality.

Risky Assumptions

In fact, when planning for retirement, many people make assumptions that reveal a total lack of understanding, which can be dangerous. Actuaries say people are living longer — one spouse will survive to age 100 in approximately five to 15 of every 100 couples. This is good news, for certain, but many people plan only with an average life span in mind. This runs counter to the latest statistical evidence that says that of half of the married couples age 65 in 2005, both partners are likely to survive to age 80. This means that too few people are considering the probability that they'll live another 15 years, struggling financially in later years because they budgeted only to the average life span. The solution: You've got to consider ways to extend your savings, or find alternate money that can kick in later in life.

Too few couples acknowledge that one partner will outlive the other by a significant period of time — a mistaken belief to be sure, actuaries say. A lot of the surviving partners are going to be women (57 percent of Americans over age 65 are women, 43 percent are men).

It is a mistake to plan based on your current situation while failing to focus on the needs of the survivor. Instead, plan as a couple, making sure that the surviving spouse will be well provided for. If pension income is available, use a joint and survivor option. Also consider the possibility of a survivor annuity, life insurance, or a trust to help protect the surviving spouse.

The timing of retirement is not always up to the individual (nearly four in 10 people retire before they plan or want to). Many people in their 60s and beyond plan to work in retirement. You may be able to phase into retirement or work part-time. This is certainly an admirable goal; however, it is important not to rely on it solely when planning. Disability, family members in poor health, and unforeseen changes in the labor market and demand can easily make employment opportunities difficult or unrealistic. Statistics reveal that more than six million older Americans are poor or nearly poor. Almost 30 percent of older unmarried women fall into this category, compared to 8 percent of older married couples. A simple factor we don't always take into consideration is inflation's effect on prices — especially if the money we've got isn't growing as fast.

Filling the Gap

How do you keep the good times rolling, when working is not an option? Figure out the guaranteed monthly income (Social Security, pension benefits) that will be received, no matter how long you or your partner live. If your guaranteed, regular monthly income doesn't cover your more realistic, projected, regular living expenses, consider an immediate annuity to provide added income — guaranteed for life. You can buy an annuity to start at any age — immediately on retirement, or later. Alternatively, you can buy longevity insurance — with income to start much later, say at age 85. This will allow you to safely plan to use most of your other assets by age 85, when the longevity insurance starts to provide monthly payments.

Remember, buying an annuity is not right for everyone. A good guide on this topic is "Making Your Money Last for a Lifetime," a booklet from the Women's Institute for a Secure Retirement (WISER) (www.

wiserwomen.org) and the Actuarial Foundation (www. actuarialfoundation.org).

Assuming that unpleasant and unexpected events (including illness, the premature death of a spouse, or the need for long-term care) will only happen to others is, of course, unwise. In 2004 the cost for a semiprivate room in a nursing home averaged $61,685 per year. The average cost for a home health aide was $18 per hour; if just four hours of care were needed each day, it would add up to $26,000 per year.

Private, long-term care insurance is a good solution for middle-income Americans with savings that could be wiped out; it can help protect the surviving spouse. Without such insurance, savings sometimes are used to care for the first to become ill and die, leaving the survivor with little but Social Security.

For many people, particularly those without pensions, their house is their largest asset and may be their only source of significant savings. Many people want to continue to live in their home and will own it free and clear by the time they retire. They may need added income to live comfortably. Reverse mortgages are an option that allow you to get monthly income based on the value of your home, while you stay in it; the payments can be guaranteed for life.

Many people have already paid off mortgages and don't have much debt at 60. If you're making substantial payments on outstanding debt, pay it off and be sure to think about how doing that will impact your finances in retirement.

Eyeing the Bottom Line

If you don't already have a plan in place by age 60, it's not too late to start. As part of your planning, it is essential to understand the risks and uncertainties during later years, along with corresponding financial products that can be used to insure those risks. With this knowledge, you can then decide which options work for you.

Seven Financial Rules for Retirees

by Mark Cussen, CFP, CMFC

Mark P. Cussen, CFP, CMFC, has over 17 years of experience in the financial industry and has worked as a stockbroker, life insurance agent, income tax preparer, and loan officer. He has published numerous articles on several Web sites, including www.investopedia.com, www.moneycrashers.com, www.primerates.com, and www.ehow.com. He also works as an educator for the U.S. military and is currently learning to day-trade at the Online Trading Academy.

I f you're like most retirees, you have probably spent a good portion of your life trying to accumulate a nest egg that will allow you to live the kind of life that you want after you stop working. Of course, some of you have been more successful than others, but your attitude about money and your ability to cope without a paycheck coming in will play major roles in the quality of your retirement, even if you were fortunate or adept enough to accumulate substantial wealth during your working years. The rules that I'm giving you here do not represent a concrete goal to be achieved or steps to be taken *per se*; they will merely make it easier for you to accomplish all the other things that you want to do when you retire, such as traveling, indulging in a hobby, or contributing to a worthy cause.

Rule #1: Learn What You Don't Know

If you are still clueless about how to read your financial statements, balance your investment portfolio, or perform other basic monetary tasks, then it's time to catch up. There is a plethora of free educational courses and tutorials, sponsored by governmental agencies such as FINRA and the SEC, which explain the basic tenets of insurance, investing, and retirement planning in a simple and objective fashion. Your local library and the AARP also offer many resources that can help you learn how to handle your money.

Rule #2: Beware of Predators

There are multitudes of con artists in this world who specialize in separating trusting retirees and senior citizens from their hard-earned money. Never, ever let anyone smooth-talk or intimidate you into making a major financial decision that you're not comfortable with. Beware of anyone who calls you out of the blue and asks for money for a worthy cause, especially if you've never heard of the caller or the organization he or she represents. Before you start working with a new financial adviser, verify the adviser's legitimacy by logging on to the Brokercheck service at www.finra.org, or by contacting your state insurance commissioner.

Rule #3: Diversify Your Portfolio

Numerous studies have shown that those who diversify their investments across several asset classes such as stocks, bonds, cash, and real estate are much less vulnerable to economic upheaval than those who have all their eggs in one or two baskets. If a substantial percentage of your portfolio still consists of shares of stock in your former employer, then it's probably time to reallocate some or all of those shares into a portfolio of mutual funds or other instruments. But don't count on the performance of a single fund, stock, or other security to meet your financial goals. Just ask anyone who "retired" from Enron or WorldCom.

Rule #4: Don't Be Afraid of Risk

Although prudent investing is the foundation for any

nest egg, remember that there is no such thing as a risk-free investment. Some instruments are guaranteed for principal and interest, such as government bonds and fixed annuities, but they can be vulnerable to inflation and taxes. It is probably a good idea to keep at least a small portion of your portfolio in equities, in order to maintain a hedge against future inflation. Those who keep all of their savings in CDs and money market accounts can rest easy knowing that their money is safe, but must also accept that their money will buy them less and less over time.

Rule #5: Plan Ahead and Use Common Sense

Although a certain amount of risk in your portfolio is unavoidable, this is not the time to start taking excessive or unnecessary chances with your money. If you have a hankering to dabble in commodities futures, do your homework and take some courses taught by experienced traders before you begin. You should also get your estate plan in order, if you haven't done so yet; millions of dollars are needlessly paid out of the estates of deceased persons each year to probate courts. In addition, a well-crafted estate plan can prevent unnecessary litigation and feuding among your beneficiaries and descendants, who may have very different ideas about how to distribute the assets in your estate than you do.

Rule #6: You Can't Take It With You, So Give It Away Now
Although a sound estate plan is always a smart move, this process can be greatly simplified by passing on some of what you have now. This not only makes planning for the future easier, but it can also give you the satisfaction of seeing your gifts being used and enjoyed by your family or other beneficiary in the manner that you intended. This axiom doesn't just apply to the wealthy; even those of modest means probably own some items of either monetary or sentimental value that they may want to impart before they go. Accelerating your estate plan can also help your beneficiaries reach their own financial goals; a contribution to the college funds of your grandchildren now will go much further than the same amount bequeathed in 10 years.

Rule #7: Don't Let Money Control Your Life
Although your finances will obviously continue to impact how you live in many ways, don't let dollars and cents be the driving factor in every decision you make. I'm not encouraging fiscal irresponsibility here; I'm just saying that life is short and money isn't all

that matters. Of course, you still need to use common sense and diversify your portfolio carefully, but don't be afraid to spend some of what you've accumulated, either. If you've always dreamed of owning a sailboat but could never afford one, then this might be a good time to explore the financial impact of purchasing one and perhaps living on it for a while. Retirement represents your last chance to do the things that you've always wanted to do but never could before.

23

What to Look for in Financial Advisers

by Jim Yih

Jim Yih is a financial expert who puts financial education programs in the workplace. For more information, you can visit his Web site, www.RetireHappy.ca, or his award-winning blog, www.RetireHappyBlog.ca.

I have found that when people reach retirement they sometimes look to change financial advisers. While this used to be common practice, many investors found that the grass wasn't necessarily greener on the other side. The current thinking is to stay with one's current adviser as long as he or she provides the best reason to stay — excellent service. A good adviser will add value to your financial picture. For me, it all boils down to two basic points: 1) Do you trust this person with your financial affairs? 2) Does this person demonstrate some acceptable level of competence?

The fact is your financial adviser is getting paid to help you make good financial and investment decisions. Many investors are questioning the credibility and ability of their advisers. Are these investors justified in thinking this way? Or are they just looking for excuses to make changes?

The only way to determine if your financial advisers are worth their compensation is to look at a number of criteria, including:

1. **Education.** Education of an adviser is an absolutely crucial criteria to determine competence. Good education is often measured by designations. Letters behind the name of an adviser show you that these people have some level of dedication, discipline, and commitment to the industry and their profession. The unfortunate part is there are some advisers that have much of the theoretical knowledge — or what I call book knowledge — but they do not have the practical experience and ability to translate theory into reality. While education is important, make sure you ask your adviser or potential advisers what they are doing to keep up their educational requirements. If your adviser is keeping up, he or she should be able to answer this

question pretty easily. You'll want someone who is really passionate about being an adviser — not just as a way of making money but because he or she really enjoys retirement planning. That passion goes a long way in an adviser achieving a high level of commitment to his or her educational goals.

2. Experience. Find out how long your adviser has been in business. An adviser with experience often really understands the practical application of theory to reality. There is an old saying in the investment industry that if you make it past three years, then you will last a lifetime. Unfortunately, many financial advisers do not make it past the first three years in this business.

3. Independence. There are some financial advisers that work for large financial institutions and will promote and sell those institution's products. Other advisers have more independence and will promote and sell the products of many financial institutions. It's important to ask yourself, "Who does my financial adviser work for? Do they work for me or do they work for a financial institution?" This is my personal bias, but an adviser that only sells one brand or one company's product is more likely to have a conflict of interest.

4. **Big-picture thinking.** Some financial advisers are really glorified salespeople trying to peddle the latest product. How can you blame them, it is how they make a living. After all, any business is about selling products or services to people who need them. However, in the financial business, there are many financial advisers who provide a lot more than just products. They provide the advice behind the products. Investors may find value added when their adviser goes beyond picking investments to give them good financial, tax, estate, or retirement advice. In fact, good advice in these areas is worth a lot more than you think. Take the time to think about whether your financial adviser has helped you save money in taxes, reduce your interest on debt, manage your cash flow, increase your income, etc. Too many financial advisers are selling investments without creating a retirement or financial plan. This is wrong!

5. **Communication.** Every relationship, whether it is a marriage, friendship, or a client-adviser relationship, requires communication. When it's not there, you're likely to feel neglected. How does your financial adviser communicate with you? Does he or she send out newsletters? Does he call you from time to time?

Does she send you reminders for review? Does he hold seminars? These are just some of the different forms of communication. If an adviser values your business, he should be communicating with you in some way, shape, or form. I always suggest that you talk to your adviser about your expectations for communication. Often it is unmet expectations that can create problems between you and your adviser.

This list may not be exhaustive, but it does provide a basic guideline of some of the things to consider if you are looking to hire a new financial adviser. The bottom line is that a good financial adviser should have the time, expertise, knowledge, resources, and tools to properly give advice and manage your money.

24

Managing Retirement Wealth without a Crystal Ball

by Julie Jason

Julie Jason manages retirement portfolios as principal of Jackson, Grant Investment Advisers (www.jacksongrant.us). Her latest book, *Managing Retirement Wealth: An Expert Guide to Personal Portfolio Management in Good Times and Bad*, launched as an Amazon "hot new release in personal finance" in November 2011. Her fifth book, AARP® *Retirement Survival Guide*, was recognized by *Booklist* (American Library Association) as a Top Ten Business Book for 2010 and received the 2010 EIFLE Award (Excellence in Financial Literacy Education); the 2010 International Book Award for Personal Finance; the 2010 National Best Books Award for Personal Finance; and the 2011 Axiom Business Book Gold Medal for Retirement Planning.

Wouldn't it be handy to start off retirement with a crystal ball? If we could predict tomorrow's markets, we could buy at the bottom and sell before a decline.

Since our earthly stock of crystal balls was depleted

centuries ago, today's investors are handicapped by not being able to see into the future.

Another path to retirement security is to accept and manage risk as an essential element of investing.

The process, which I call "personal portfolio management" and describe in *Managing Retirement Wealth*, is based on the premise that we cannot make certain what is uncertain, that mistakes will be made in assumptions, and that while risk cannot be avoided, it can be measured, monitored, and managed.

Consider these points:

1. Accept that uncertainty is an essential element of every investment.

2. Accept that you will make bad decisions from time to time. No one has a perfect investment record. Instead of trying to achieve the unachievable, focus on finding and correcting mistakes. What is a mistake? An investment that does not meet expectations. . . An assumption that proves to be wrong . . .

3. In order to set expectations, you need to think about what you want to achieve for yourself and your

family in the time that you have to devote to investing for retirement.

4. Frame your goals in terms of personal consumption. How much of your savings, or capital, are you consuming for current living expenses? If you are able to limit consumption to interest and dividends, while preserving and growing capital, you are ahead of the game. Bad or volatile markets will have less effect on you.

5. Think of your retirement assets not as individual stocks and bonds but as a portfolio that is the sum of its parts — think in terms of the big picture. How is each element of the portfolio working to help you meet your retirement goals?

6. Define how much risk you want to take. Do you want to assume general market risk, as measured by the S&P 500 Index? Or a higher or lower level of risk? The measure will help you put things in context when it comes to reviewing your portfolio.

7. Once reasonable objectives are determined, decisions can be implemented. Then, start paying close attention to the results of your decisions.

Ultimately, the key to success is correcting course when you find yourself off track.

Be careful, however, of doing what many investors do: evaluating progress by comparing this month's statement to last month's. Looking at whether you are ahead or behind in this way has the advantage of being simple, but it stops short of putting things into risk:reward decision-making context. If the accounts are down, what do you do? If the accounts are up, should you do nothing?

Recall that Bernie Madoff, the infamous Ponzi schemer whose game came to an end in 2008, "delivered" steady returns even in down markets (by taking money from others). No stock and bond portfolio can deliver straight-line returns at all times (although inexperienced investors may think so, particularly during bubble markets).

Likewise, don't judge your happiness by measuring from valleys (lows) to peaks (highs) and peaks to valleys. If your account is down from a market high, you might set a goal of recovering your "losses" as quickly as possible (a risky strategy) – or holding on to investments until you get even (an ineffective strategy).

You don't want to lose more money trying to regain your peak value or waste time in investments that are not performing.

Reacting to Market Events

Without a good review system, it is all too easy to be compelled to action by outside events. In bubble markets, which you will see again during your lifetime, many otherwise conservative investors can be drawn into highly speculative trading because they don't want to be left out while others are profiting. During bear markets, normally cautious investors can be spooked into pulling out of the market at the worst time, often without realizing that they are engaging in the risky practice of market timing. It is of utmost importance to remember your own goals and not to bother with anyone else's.

A Final Word

Placing retirement investing within the personal portfolio management/decision-making framework calls for setting objectives, defining practical metrics and possible action steps, and monitoring results, all of which are fundamental to achieving positive outcomes.

The idea is to anticipate rather than react to the market, the news, and anything that can influence you into making inopportune decisions.

25

Four Emotions to Manage When Maintaining Your Nest Egg

by Aaron W. Smith, RFC

Aaron Smith, RFC, is a Registered Financial Consultant, radio host, motivational speaker, and author of In the Black: Live Faithfully, Prosper Financially: The Ultimate 9-Step Plan For Financial Fitness. He is the founder and president of the Richmond, Virginia — headquartered AW Smith Financial Group. Smith has been featured in numerous media outlets, including Black Enterprise, NAIFA's Advisor Today, Ebony, The Register, the Atlanta Post, Investment News, USA Today, the Richmond Times-Dispatch, Financial Advisor, Virginia Business, and Dow Jones Newswire. He has appeared as a frequent guest on local ABC and CBS affiliates, and NPR, and he was featured on NBC Nightly News.

As a financial coach for 19 years, I've worked with employees and retirees from every walk of life — conducting individual consultations and leading workshops at churches, nonprofit organizations, and corporations. I've noticed that while the public has grown a lot savvier about the importance of saving before retirement, fewer people consider how to maintain their nest eggs once they stop working. That's unfortunate, because that might mean being caught off guard by four different emotions that can jettison even the best-laid retirement plans.

Fear, apathy, shame, and guilt can undermine financial self-esteem. And life tends to give us what we believe we deserve. If you're convinced that you'll never have enough to live on comfortably for the rest of your life, that can become a self-fulfilling prophecy. When it comes to money, respect your emotions: Recognize when you're experiencing them, and while they may never go away, managing them is what matters most. Let's consider how to do just that by examining these potentially damaging emotions:

1. **Fear.** This is an overarching emotion, affecting every aspect of our lives. Think of how a fearful person looks. This person might walk with his head lowered, eyes downcast, shoulders drooping. It's a physical posture that can cause an individual to miss seeing what's going on around him, and keep him from planning ahead, which is exactly what he must do in

order to live comfortably. Fear makes folks living on fixed incomes feel risk averse. That might mean, for example, keeping all of one's savings in a low-interest "safe" bank account, because investing in the stock market might always seem too risky.

Despite my advice, Gail, a well-to-do client who is a retired Baptist pastor, resists investments that would allow her to keep pace with inflation, denying herself opportunities that would allow her to continue living comfortably in retirement. She has lived like a miser, and at 68, she withdrew money from every one of her retirement accounts and deposited her cash in a low-interest Certificate of Deposit. Meanwhile, her bank is profiting from her fears — investing her money in the stock market. After three years have passed, they will return her money with a small profit, one so minimal that given the steady march of inflation, Gail will have actually lost money.

2. **Shame.** Shame makes us feel worthless. No matter how much someone might have saved up, she might feel she isn't worth much financially — and then behave in such a way as to make that true. When I think of how shame can cause self-destructive behavior, one

client in particular comes to mind. Before he became a client, Russell, a retired CEO, procrastinated about seeing me. As with all new clients, we asked him to bring in his financial statements: savings, pensions, investment, Social Security, tax returns, and secured and unsecured debts.

Shame made it difficult for Russell to show me his financial documents. For two years, he kept making and breaking appointments. When he finally showed up, he dumped a stack of paperwork onto my desk, saying, "Aaron, let me tell you a secret. That stack of paper is what has kept me from coming here." I learned that over the course of his decades-long career, Russell had earned over $8 million, but he had little to show for it in retirement. He didn't own a home, his car was only partially paid for, and he certainly didn't have enough to continue living high on the hog.

Russell said, "My family was so proud of me getting a Harvard law degree and of my becoming a CEO. My kid's teacher asked me to come in on career day and address the class about how to become successful. I felt like a fraud. I am not successful. I'm broke. Is it too late for me to turn things around?"

Few people earn as much as Russell had, but I told him, just as I tell my other clients: it's never too late to reposition your mind and your money. Some people have more time to repair financial damage, and others have less. What's important here is that you recognize the shame and then push through. Be gentle with yourself. If gathering your paperwork evokes shame, perform the task a little bit at a time — scheduling dates and times on your calendar when you might tackle a portion of your task. It might still be difficult, but know that it's always better than living in the dark. As awareness of your financial situation becomes clearer, you will begin to take pride in your efforts to improve your circumstances. Acknowledgment that he was ashamed proved to be a major step for Russell. Ten years later, he's moved out of his penthouse apartment and is living within his means. He's become the CEO of his own life.

3. **Guilt.** This emotion can make you feel that you've done something wrong — or not done enough, despite your best efforts. I work with players in the National Basketball Association and National Football League while they're actively playing and after they retire. In their playing years, they are often the first

in their families to strike it rich, and often earn more than enough to provide cars, houses, and college educations for the close relatives they've left behind. After retirement, that high-level of generosity can be a problem. But some players continue to feel so guilty about their own good fortune as compared with the struggles of their impoverished relatives that they continue to shower them with gifts. Generosity is a virtue, but so is maintaining a retirement account. If you see yourself in this picture, my advice is to show yourself some love by holding onto your nest egg. If you refuse the next monetary request from a loved one, move through the guilt by remembering that it's not a gift, if what you're giving others hurts you.

4. **Apathy.** People think they're demonstrating their faith when they ignore the importance of holding onto their nest eggs, saying, "I'm not worried, God will provide." Sometimes I want to say, "How do you know that God isn't providing for you by sending you to a financial adviser?" I am a man of faith, and so I can say without reservation that I believe God helps those who help themselves.

To overcome apathy, take action. Confront damaging

beliefs, such as "It doesn't matter if I smoke. We're all going to die sometime." Try talking back to yourself. While it's true, for instance, that we've all got to die sometime, that date could be years from now, and no one wants to drag on miserably. So start by safeguarding your greatest asset. Join a health club, for instance, walk regularly, quit smoking, or take other self-enhancing actions. Healthier and happier, you'll feel more in control of your own life, and, while you're at it, you'll be less likely to incur major medical or hospital expenses, which can safeguard your nest egg.

I hope these stories and examples have helped you to understand that when it comes to solidifying your financial future, how you feel is not nearly as important as *how you behave*. And don't let anyone tell you that money doesn't matter. In the U.S., the almighty dollar is green, and despite what the historians say about why, I like to think that the color of our money correlates with the color of spring, a season of growth and change. Now that you're retired, there's never been a better time or reason for you to change.

Section

3

DO GOOD BY
GIVING BACK

26

The Best Years of Our Lives

by Jimmy Carter, 2002 Nobel Peace Prize Laureate

Jimmy Carter was 39th President of the United States, from 1977-1981. In 2002, he was awarded the Nobel Peace Prize for his successful mediation of the Camp David Accords in the White House in 1978 and for his "decades of untiring effort to find peaceful solutions to international conflicts, to advance democracy and human rights, and to promote economic and social development" through The Carter Center after he left office.

Few people have turned retirement into an opportunity for volunteerism with more enthusiasm than former President Jimmy Carter. Now 87, Carter is founder of the nonprofit Carter Center in Atlanta. Here he explains why he spends his time volunteering — and why he finds it so satisfying.

When I retired from the White House in 1980 (four years earlier than planned), Rosalynn and I were faced with deciding how to spend the rest of our lives. We were fairly young —

both in our 50s — and unemployed. We went directly from the White House to our home in Plains, Georgia (population 700), where we had not lived since I was elected governor.

You can imagine that this was not an easy transition. But we agreed that Plains was our home and where we wanted to stay. I had no desire to run again for public office, so we started thinking about how we could use some of the skills and experience we had acquired over the years to work on issues that had always been important to us.

We did a lot of soul-searching the first year, and out of this process came the idea for The Carter Center (www.cartercenter.org). We envisioned a nonprofit center, not affiliated with any government or political party, where we could bring people and resources together to promote peace and improve health around the world. We opened our center on the campus of Emory University in 1982 and moved into our permanent headquarters, adjacent to the newly built Jimmy Carter Library & Museum, in 1986.

Over the years, Rosalynn and I have turned retirement into another career through our work at The Carter

Center. And I have to say that our post-Presidential years have been even more fulfilling than our years in public office. On behalf of The Carter Center, we have traveled to more than 125 countries. In North Korea, Haiti, Nicaragua, Liberia, the Sudan, and other nations, we have helped resolve conflicts and defuse potentially explosive crises. We've spent weeks in remote villages in Africa, teaching residents how to eradicate Guinea worm disease and handing out free medicine to control river blindness. In other parts of Africa, we've helped farmers increase grain and corn production as much as 400 percent using simple, inexpensive agricultural practices. We've advanced human rights and helped developing countries draft master plans for development.

Rich Life

At home in the U.S., Rosalynn has continued her efforts on behalf of the mentally ill, building on her work as First Lady of Georgia and of the U.S. We've helped inner-city residents in Atlanta develop strategies to improve their lives, sharing what we've learned with more than 100 other cities. When we're not working for The Carter Center, we spend a week each year building homes with other volunteers for Habitat for Humanity in the U.S. and other countries.

All these projects have enriched my life in untold ways. I've learned things I never knew as a state senator or governor or even President. While reaching out to others, Rosalynn and I have filled our own needs to be challenged and to act as productive members of our global community.

Along the way, we've also found others seeking opportunities to lend time, experience, and resources to alleviate suffering and improve lives. For example, at The Carter Center, we pool our resources with those of our many partners — including corporations, foundations, and individuals. I've visited with employees of donors, including Merck, DuPont, and United Parcel Service, and many were moved to tears when I told them how their companies' donations have helped free villages in Africa from Guinea worm disease and river blindness or eased the struggles of a family in our own country.

Let me give you another example of how retirement has changed how we view the world. Carter Center teams have observed 85 elections in 34 countries. In 1990, we stood in line with Haitians at the polling place where, just three years earlier, dozens of people had been killed by government-sponsored terrorists while trying to vote. Many had risen in the middle of the night to walk 10 or 15 miles to stand in that same line — even though they feared for their lives. As we traveled around Port-au-Prince that day, we talked to people who had waited for hours just for the opportunity to vote — a sacred privilege that we and others often take for granted in the U.S.

We live in a land of opportunity, and our retirement from political life has opened a whole new world of excitement and challenges. We've also been able to spend more time with our children and grandchildren and to enjoy ourselves with new hobbies and interests. I learned to downhill ski when I was 62. We have taken up bird-watching, and I've spent a lot of time in the woodworking shop in my garage, making furniture for family and friends. Rosalynn and I and several family members have climbed the Himalayas and have reached the tops of Mt. Kilimanjaro and Mt. Fuji. We fish in many places and relax in our cabin in the Georgia mountains.

For us, retirement has not been the end but a new beginning. We hope to spend many more years actively making the most of the rest of our lives.

27

Enrich Your Life:
Push Back Against the Box

by Bob Lowry

Bob Lowry was a management consultant to several hundred radio stations before retiring in 2001. He has written two books, authors a successful retirement blog, and lives with his wife in Scottsdale, Arizona.

For the last four years, I have done something I never imagined I would do, before or after retirement. I became involved in an activity so alien to my background and comfort level that it can best be described as pushing back against the box I was in at the time. When I began, there were serious doubts about my ability to carry out the task with even a modicum of success. A year into the process, my involvement took a major step forward in a way that dramatically increased the risk of failure and a risk of physical danger.

Four years ago, I became involved with prison ministry. I began to act as a mentor — a spiritual guide and sounding board to men who were either still in prison or were just about to be released. Trust me, up until that point I had zero involvement with this segment of society. Like most of us, my attitude toward prisoners was they probably got what they deserved. They were paying the cost for bad choices or for being unlucky enough to be born in a poor environment. They were invisible as people; they were a stereotype.

The first exposure came when my church asked me to write to a fellow who was in state prison. He had been in jail for most of his life. He had no family support and had no visitors for over two years. With two more years to go on his latest sentence, I began to exchange letters with him. The first few were very difficult. I had absolutely no idea what to say or not say. What questions should I ask? What should I not ask? Would he even bother to write back?

He did respond and was overjoyed to have anyone communicating with him. Even when I made it clear his situation was impossible for me to truly relate to, he didn't care. He just needed someone to give him hope and a little bit of attention. We continued to exchange letters for over a year until he felt comfortable enough in the relationship to ask me to visit him inside the prison.

Okay, this wasn't something I had bargained for. I've seen enough prison movies to know that bad things happen behind the barbed wire. I figured there would be a paperwork screwup and I'd not be allowed to leave. Writing to someone was one thing, but actually going into a prison to meet someone I knew only through letters? I began to generate every reason why I couldn't do this.

I went. I thought of how I'd feel if I had been locked up and no one had come to see me in nearly three years. I figured people visit inmates all the time so I'd be fine. But, when the bus taking me into the prison yard rolled past the two tall, steel-gray gates, the barbed wire, the guard towers, and the patrolling dogs, I got very nervous.

It worked out just fine. Actually, the fellow I went to see was so nervous he hadn't eaten in two days. He was worried I wouldn't show up and his cellmates would ridicule him. He worried his only chance to talk with someone who wasn't dressed in an orange jumpsuit would not happen. Once we sat down together, I think he talked virtually nonstop for the 90-minute visit. I went back a few months later to see him again. A few months after that, he was released from prison and is doing fine.

The reaction of that fellow to the simplest human contact of letter writing led me to make another commitment. Two years ago, I agreed to become a mentor and friend of a convict for a period of six months starting on the day he is released from prison. This program involves substantially more time and effort. As someone's mentor, I am expected to talk with him on the phone at least four times a week and visit him at the halfway house a minimum of once a week for the first four months. I am also expected to help him develop a budget and stay away from old friends and habits. I help him get a job, buy him some new clothes, drive him to medical appointments, and meet with his parole officer on a regular basis. I attend church services with him and help him in his faith walk. I am the person he calls when he worries he's about to make a mistake.

This experience has been absolutely fabulous. Both fellows I have mentored have successfully completed the six-month program. Both have become employed and positive members of society. Both have overcome society's attitude that once a convict, always a convict. The barriers we erect to keep these guys from succeeding are enormous. To their credit, they have overcome all the obstacles put in their way.

Why this long story about prison ministry? I want to give you a very personal example of pushing back against the limits that we often set for ourselves. Volunteering your time and skills can help you face some of your fears. It can push you to grow.

Are you uncomfortable around children or homeless people? How do you feel about domestic violence? Do you avoid people who are dying? Do you believe all convicts are not to be trusted and are destined to end up back behind bars?

Are you willing to confront those perceptions by becoming involved with the very people you fear or are uncomfortable being near? Are you prepared to learn something new about yourself and the world we live in?

What I ask is that you think about your self-constructed box and how it might limit you. "Thinking outside the box" is a cliché, but it doesn't make the statement any less powerful. There is a whole world needing what you have to give. What better time to discover it than when you retire?

28

A New Dimension to Our Lives

by Bill Birnbaum

Bill Birnbaum is the author of A *Lifetime of Small Adventures: Stories of Adventure, Misadventure, and Lessons Learned Along the Way.* He writes a blog at www.AdventureRetirement.com, and lives in Sisters, Oregon, with his adventurous wife, Wendy, a red kayak, and a well-worn pair of hiking boots.

My wife, Wendy, and I had promised ourselves that, when we retired, ours would be an active, adventurous retirement. In fact, we avoided using the word "retirement." Instead, we'd refer to "a new dimension to our lives."

We both expected that our "new dimension" would involve more than simply selecting a pretty town with a small population and a mountain range nearby. There was also the question of "what will we do when we get there?" Wendy, especially, wanted to do volunteer work

— to help people and to benefit society.

In the spring of 2005, we attended a retirement fair on the campus of a nearby university. There, we met a recruiter from the United States Peace Corps. A 20-minute conversation with the recruiter was all we needed — we were interested. We spent that evening reading over the Peace Corps publications. Within two days, we were filling out our applications.

The organization warns applicants, "Don't assume you'll be accepted into the Peace Corps. Some people aren't. Don't quit your job or sell your house." Allan, our Peace Corps recruiter, offered us a very specific warning about the Peace Corps' medical department. He said that it was a bureaucracy, and especially tough when it came to screening seniors. Seems that while the Peace Corps recruiters were working very hard to develop volunteers among the senior community, the Peace Corps' medical department was working very hard to reject them. Allan warned us, "For sure, don't sell your home."

In spite of this warning, Wendy shut down her law practice, and I, my consulting practice. And we sold our home.

The Peace Corps approved Wendy's application quickly. But mine got hung up in the all-powerful bureaucracy of the Peace Corps' medical department. Seems that, when I took my medical exam, one of my three blood pressure readings was a bit high. So my doctor prescribed a blood pressure medicine. Because of this, the Peace Corps' medical department required that I take a whole series of tests. No matter that the various tests showed that I was fine, the Peace Corps' medical department kept asking for more and more tests. They seemed impossible to satisfy. This hassle with the medical department dragged on for many months. Finally, they rejected my application.

Actually, we took this news pretty well. We didn't resent the personal commitment we had made to the Peace Corps — selling our home, closing down Wendy's law practice and my consulting practice, and putting everything we owned in storage. Instead of looking back, we looked forward. We both agreed, "Okay, if the Peace Corps won't have us, we'll create our own volunteer experience."

Though it would be more complicated to find our own volunteer opportunity, we were especially enthusiastic about doing so. As Wendy explained, "We now have a blank canvas on which we can paint any picture we choose."

We immediately began planning our "new dimension." Wendy suggested, "Let's go to South America; there we'll have the opportunity to immerse ourselves in the Spanish language and to learn about, and travel in, another continent."

"That sounds fine to me," I agreed.

Researching each of South America's countries, we decided on Peru — for a couple of reasons. First, it's a poor country with many needs; we figured we'd likely have our choice of volunteer opportunities there. And Peru has many indigenous people — 12 million of a total population of 28 million. This would, no doubt, prove culturally interesting. We were set — we'd go to Peru.

As Wendy was relatively new to the Spanish language, we decided to begin our sojourn in Peru with a few weeks of language school. Searching on the Internet, we found an excellent language school in Arequipa, Peru's second-largest city. In addition to one-on-one language instruction, the school offered "home stay," that is, they'd arrange for us to live with a local family. We appreciated the idea that home stay would offer us a great orientation both to the Spanish language and to Peruvian culture.

With that settled, we next turned our attention to potential volunteer opportunities. With some online research, I learned of an organization called ADEA Abancay. Its mission was to boost the economy in the town of Abancay and in the even poorer surrounding region of Apurímac in the Peruvian Andes. It did so by providing consultation to entrepreneurs. Hmmm . . . business consulting. Right up my alley. I began an e-mail correspondence with a fellow named Danilo Córdova, the head of consulting at ADEA. He told me that he could use my help in consulting to entrepreneurs.

I said to Wendy, "This opportunity with ADEA looks interesting. But I don't know what volunteer opportunities might be available to you in Abancay."

She said, "If the opportunity with ADEA is of interest to you, let's go to Abancay. I'm sure I'll find a volunteer opportunity there."

I sent Danilo an e-mail and told him we'd travel to Abancay to meet with him and explore the volunteer opportunity that he'd offered me. The plan was we'd fly from Los Angeles, California, to Arequipa, Peru. There we'd study Spanish for six weeks, then travel 16 hours by bus to Abancay. In Abancay, I'd meet with Danilo and, potentially, work with ADEA as a volunteer business consultant.

During the six weeks we lived with the family in one of Arequipa's middle-class neighborhoods, studying Spanish, we developed a wonderful relationship with them. Following our six-week stay there, we traveled by bus to Abancay. I met with Danilo and decided to work with him at ADEA.

Wendy literally walked around town knocking on doors, using her "beginner Spanish" in her search for volunteer work. She landed an assignment helping kids in an after-school program. Through that work, she developed wonderfully warm relationships both with the kids and also with her coworkers.

Two years after completing our volunteer work, we returned to Peru. The purpose of our trip was to attend the wedding of the son of the family with whom we had lived in Arequipa. During that same trip, we also returned to Abancay. There, we celebrated the high school graduation of three of the girls with whom Wendy had worked.

Our Peruvian friends refer to Wendy and me as their American family. We, in turn, refer to them as our Peruvian family. Indeed, our move to Peru, upon retirement, added an exciting and significant new dimension to our lives.

29

"It's Not Where You've Been, But Where You're Going"

by Rick Koca

Rick Koca is the founder of StandUp For Kids, a national all-volunteer (at least 99 percent) nonprofit organization solely committed to ending the cycle of youth homelessness.

I was the CEO of StandUp For Kids for more than 20 years. During that time it grew from one program in San Diego to more than 44 programs in 25 states, making it the largest nonprofit organization helping homeless and street youth in America. A year ago I retired from my position as CEO to spend more time with my three children, seven grandchildren, and a great-grandson in colorful Colorado.

I am the second of nine children from parents with meager earnings. Raised in Nebraska, I donned the Navy's blue uniform at the tender age of 17 after graduating from high school, and I pursued this adventurous career for the next 30 years. I worked hard and it showed; I was promoted 13 times through 17 pay grades. Maybe that doesn't sound like much, but fewer than 1 out of 10,000 ever achieve this distinction. I knew what success was for me and how to achieve it; I'd set my goals and make plans to attain them. No, things didn't always go as planned, but I was committed and determined to reach my success.

Children Living on the Streets

A year before I left the Navy, I became aware of the homeless youth problem in San Diego and in our country more generally. To say it devastated me would certainly be an understatement. Here I'd just spent more than two-thirds of my life fighting for a country that I believed in, and we had children living on the streets. No, we had hundreds of thousands of children living on the streets. How could this be?

Nothing in my past 30 years with the Navy prepared me to start a program for homeless and street youth. First of all, I knew nothing about nonprofits, homeless youth, fund-raising, or a board of directors, or, okay you get the picture. . . .The only thing I knew for sure was that children should not have to live on the streets, eat out of dumpsters, or prostitute themselves just to survive. Actually, people laughed at me when I told them what I was going to do when I retired. They told me all the things that I already knew, or, in reality, all of the things I didn't know about starting a nonprofit.

For me, it wasn't about what I didn't know, but about what I knew. I certainly knew that children, in the richest nation on earth, didn't have to live on the streets, eat out of dumpsters, or sleep under bridges. Starting StandUp For Kids wasn't easy but with a few close friends and backpacks full of food and hygiene products we began walking the streets. It was never easy meeting new kids; they usually wondered why we wanted to help, and we often wondered how we could.

When we'd meet new kids, the first thing that we asked them was, "If there is one thing that I could do for you today, what would that be?" The question gave us a place to start, to see where they thought they were, and then we could work from there. At first, the answer would be something simple, such as a bottle of water. We never supposed that we knew what they needed. It was to become a question that we'd ask them regularly to see how they were progressing. As time passed, they would ask for help in obtaining their birth certificate so they could get an ID, or a GED, or a job, and then an apartment. These small steps took months and, in some cases, years!

"I Was Crying and I Could Hear Other Kids Crying"

I remember meeting a young man named Brian on the streets of San Diego. He was 15, from Arkansas, and had been living on the streets for several months. We gave him some food and clean clothes. Over the weeks and months that followed, I came to know Brian very well. He was a good lad, but addicted to meth and as hard as we tried, we couldn't get him to stop using. When Brian was 17, he and I were being interviewed by a San Diego newspaper reporter. I didn't hear the question that she asked Brian, but I'll never forget what I heard him say: "I can remember nights in my squat when I would be rolled up in a ball, with my thumb in my mouth. I would be crying and I could hear other kids crying and I was praying that I would go to sleep and not wake up in the morning." I looked at him and was fighting to hold back the tears. I wondered how did we, the richest nation in the world, get to such a place where we let our children live — no, *die* — on the streets! It's reported that more than 13 homeless youth die on the streets every day; they die from abuse, disease, and suicide.

She Was Keeping the Dog

In Los Angeles, a young man named David told me that when he was 14 his mother had told him that she could only afford him or the dog and she was keeping the dog! And, a young girl named Angel told me, "When I was 10, my mother chose crack over me!"

In 2006, Virgin Unite, the nonprofit foundation of the Virgin Group — established in 2005 by Sir Richard Branson, chose StandUp For Kids as their first charity partner in the United States. In the past five years, their leadership, financial support, and gifts in-kind have been tremendously invaluable, not only to StandUp For Kids, but to many nonprofits who help at-risk youth in the United States. Especially noteworthy was their assistance in July of 2007, along with the financial and leadership support of Virgin Mobile USA, in having the month of November designated by Congress and the Senate as National Homeless Youth Awareness Month.

Light at the End of the Tunnel

I like to tell people, "If you don't see the light at the end of the tunnel, maybe you're going in the wrong direction!" I believe that if you know what success is for yourself, and you have goals and plans to achieve that personal success, then there *is* a light at the end of the tunnel, and you know you're going the right way. It's an awesome feeling knowing what success is going to look like even before you get there.

I like to say that my favorite word is IMPOSSIBLE. If you really look at this word, it simply says *I'm Possible.* We are all possible if we believe we are.

Next year I'll be 70; as the years have passed, I've repeatedly returned to one of my first thoughts when I started StandUp For Kids — that our children should not have to die alone on the streets.

Maybe that's all I still know now!
I'm Possible, Rick

30

Embrace Life

by Pamela Good

Pamela Good is a graduate of the University of Michigan and has always been an entrepreneur at heart. She started her first business at the age of 21 — Farmington Computer Services, a business that specialized in client company payroll and production of financial statements for certified public accountants. After years in the workforce, she left to raise her family. In 1999 she volunteered to help with a coat drive benefitting a Detroit public school. That day her eyes were opened to the vast deficiencies in public education. She began putting together enrichment activities that led to her becoming the cofounder and executive director of Beyond Basics (www.beyondbasics.org), a nonprofit organization that helps at-risk children in the Metropolitan Detroit public schools to develop fundamental educational skills and prepares them to lead productive and meaningful lives.

L ife has a way of showing us who we really are as individuals and collectively as a society. The story of our lives is like a mirror reflecting back our actions and displaying the level of truth we possess. If we are paying attention and we take responsibility, we can change everything. With this realization, I made a conscious effort to increase the soulful part of me, seeking those things eternal, to choose truth and embrace life.

As I moved through decades of adulthood and retired from the workforce, it became clear to me that growing my spirit was the ultimate goal. How better to grow spirit than to take action in its attributes, things unseen? In fact, the only way to see spirit is through demonstration, through action. For us to see courage, someone must be courageous. For us to see love, someone must behave lovingly. As I practiced these parts of my spirit, each part became stronger. As I confronted my fears and stepped out with courage, I became more courageous. As I turned away from worrying and walked forward with faith, my faith grew, making it easier for me to step out again.

I found that as I turned my life over to spirit, spirit took over my life. I was presented with opportunity after opportunity to take action, and in doing so, many beautiful things have come to life for me and for many, many others because of it. From being courageous, having faith, and acting on what seemed like the right thing to do, an organization called Beyond Basics came to life.

Twelve years ago I delivered coats to one inner-city Detroit public school. Being in the school allowed me to see the vast deficiencies in public education and made me aware that many children were living in extreme poverty and conditions that were totally unacceptable. With concern for children and the belief that someone should help, I left that day saying, "I will do more."

For two years, with the help of others who joined in this mission, we ran pilot programs with groups of students in one school, testing ideas to see how the children responded. Each trial produced the same result, and it was the children's enthusiasm that provided the catalyst to create and grow the organization.

Motivated by the response of participating students, in February 2002, we incorporated as a nonprofit for the sole purpose of reaching more children. That September, Beyond Basics established its first on-site publishing center and formalized many other programs. Since then, our publishing center, our one-on-one reading tutoring program (where we get children reading at grade level in six weeks using certified tutors), our Art with the Masters classes, and our mentoring partnership program have touched the lives of thousands of children in kindergarten through 12th grade.

After all these years of working with children in the lowest performing schools in the city, what amazes me most is the resilience of the human spirit. It is why I know "there is hope for Detroit." There are thousands of children and people in this city who need help, who need us.

I realize at this moment it is difficult for many to see "these diamonds in the rough." These little diamonds have forgotten their own brilliance; as with all of us,it is easy for these children to believe they are their circumstances. That is one way we help; we are their mirror reflecting back their greatness. We show them in so many ways who they really are and what they are capable of being and doing. They soak up these affirmations like a dry soil after a strong rain. The change that happens within them will power this city in new directions. This new foundation is filled with spirit.

There is hope for and in Detroit! I witness it every day.

When you exercise attributes of the spirit, they grow! We are growing hope, courage, faith, and love.

I stepped out for children who had forgotten who they were and in doing so, I found myself. What I imagined and desired for others has come to me. As we look for spirit, it opens itself up to us. It is always there waiting for us to acknowledge its presence.

For many retirees who seek a renewed purpose in their lives, volunteering at a nonprofit — or even starting one — can help them find their own truth and embrace life in a multitude of meaningful ways.

This organization has required me to be better, to be stronger, believing when no one else did. It has taught me to walk through my fears and stand on my emotions. Many others have joined in this mission, responding to the call of these beautiful children and finding themselves along the way.

31

For LGBT Retirees and Their Allies, Volunteer Opportunities Abound!

by Michael Adams

Michael Adams is the executive director of SAGE — Services and Advocacy for GLBT Elders. SAGE is the oldest and largest organization in the country dedicated to transforming the LGBT aging experience. Prior to joining SAGE, he was the director of Education and Public Affairs for Lambda Legal, and before that, he served as associate director of the ACLU's Lesbian and Gay Rights Project, and then as deputy legal director at Lambda Legal. A graduate of Stanford Law School and Harvard College, Adams has taught law school courses on sexual orientation and gender identity and has served on advisory councils for AARP, the American Society on Aging, and the New York City Department for the Aging, among others. He has appeared on hundreds of media programs, including *Larry King Live*, *The O'Reilly Factor*, and *Hannity & Colmes*, and NPR's *Morning Edition* and *All Things Considered*. He has twice been named one of the "100 most influential gay men and lesbians" by *Out* magazine.

As the executive director of Services & Advocacy for Gay, Lesbian, Bisexual & Transgender Elders (SAGE) — the country's oldest and largest organization working on behalf of LGBT older people — I know from firsthand experience one way that hundreds of older people make their retirement years especially rich and fulfilling. They volunteer! The work that SAGE does on behalf of LGBT elders would not be possible were it not for the hundreds of volunteers — many of them retired — who contribute their time and talent.

The elders SAGE serves benefit immeasurably from our amazing volunteer corps. But our volunteers get at least as much out of volunteering as SAGE elders do. According to the Institute for Volunteering Research, retirees are attracted to give back to their communities for many reasons. Some miss the structure and schedule of the workplace. Others like volunteering for a break from the routines of a lifetime of paid work. Volunteering is a great way to meet people, to keep the mind and body active, and to make a powerful contribution to society. It's also a great way to feel — and be — appreciated.

There are many different ways to volunteer. One need go no further than the Giving Back page at AARP.org to find 65 fun ways to volunteer with just a click of the mouse. You can assist teachers and schoolchildren, help grandkids (without writing a check!), honor fallen soldiers, fight hunger, support the environment, volunteer abroad, and so much more. You can become a foster grandparent and mentor children in need of positive influences. If you like getting your hands dirty, plant trees near the homes of family and friends. You can volunteer to make a healthy grocery list and take an elderly neighbor shopping. You can volunteer to read to children at schools. If your volunteer time is limited, send a thank-you card to your local fire or police station for their work in the community.

For LGBT retirees and their allies, volunteer opportunities abound. You'll make a huge difference volunteering with an LGBT community organization, most of which literally could not exist without volunteer support. The Los Angeles Gay & Lesbian Center, the country's largest LGBT organization, reports that since 1997 its 3,000 annual volunteers have contributed more than $11 million in time and services.

AIDS organizations like Gay Men's Health Crisis rely on volunteers across the country each year for AIDS Walks that raise millions of dollars to support critically needed service programs. Bilingual volunteers are needed across LGBT organizations. LGBT youth organizations need volunteers for things like tutoring, career counseling, and recreation activities.

For those who want to practice their public speaking — and those who are already hams and don't need any practice — many LGBT organizations across the country have speakers' bureaus and enlist volunteers to speak everywhere, from schools to county fairs. Sometimes volunteering comes with glamour and great food! The San Diego LGBT Community Center's annual Dining Out for Life brings together more than 100 restaurants to raise funds for needed programs and relies on foodie volunteers called Restaurant Ambassadors.

One of SAGE's best-known volunteer opportunities is our Friendly Visitor program, where individuals sign up for weekly visits to a homebound elder. Friendly visitors often form fast friendships with the elders they visit.

Volunteerism can offer unique opportunities for leadership. SAGE relies on a team of extraordinarily dedicated volunteers, including retirees, who serve on its Board of Directors, providing the organization with strategic direction and helping with programmatic fund-raising.

Sometimes volunteering can be about making the world a better place by advocating for change. SAGE Advocates testify at public hearings, meet with elected officials, and engage in the American tradition of rabble-rousing to make sure that laws and public policies take account of the needs of all elders, including LGBT elders.

Some show just how committed they are by putting in the volunteer version of "sweat equity." Eyal Feldman is a SAGE volunteer who takes part in an annual marathon swim, asking friends and family for financial support for each mile he swims. Last summer, Eyal swam seven miles across Lake Mead, at the foot of the Hoover Dam, and raised more than $8,000 for SAGE! In the interest of full disclosure, Eyal is nowhere near retirement age. Not everyone can swim across a large body of water, but I bet there is a retiree out there who can beat Eyal's record!

Few things during retirement are more rewarding than volunteering. A blogger on AARP's Giving Back Web page summed it up when she wrote: "This is the BEST I've done (other than granbabies) . . . I REALLY URGE all those physically capable of volunteering @ least 1x/ month doing any type of work they've always wanted to do . . . anyone can find their niche close by. As Nike used to say 'Just Do It!!!'"

32

Retire and ReServe: Because You Should

by Mary S. Bleiberg

Mary S. Bleiberg arrived at ReServe after a decade at the After School Corporation (TASC). As vice president of Policy and Program Development, she helped to raise nearly $500 million in public and private funds, and to create sustainable service and funding strategies that have led to a dramatic growth in the quality and availability of after-school services. Prior to working at TASC, Bleiberg served in a variety of government and not-for-profit organizations, including Safe Horizon, Urban Pathways, the New York City Human Resources Administration, City Volunteer Corps, and the Mayor's Office of Midtown Enforcement.

Two years ago, a group of international thought leaders were asked to come up with a descriptor for Americans over 55. They were unable, after two days, to agree on a suitable term. Some words were seen as too pejorative ("old," "elderly," "aged"), or too broad ("mature," "experienced," "seasoned"), or patronizing ("golden agers," "senior citizens"). What about calling them "retired" or "retirees"? These terms turned out not to be applicable to a large and growing proportion of, well, older adults.

What they — or we — decide to call this age group is not as important as what Americans over 55 decide to do with the rest of their lives, and since we're living longer, that has come to mean many more years. Given the large numbers, relative wealth, high educational levels, and health status of Americans born between 1946 and 1964 compared to those born before or after, it is no exaggeration to say that the future of our country may well depend on what this group decides to do with the 20 years after they "retire" from their primary careers.

Many of us look forward to using our retirement for travel, recreation, and the leisurely pursuit of new and old interests. But 20 years is a long time for so many people with so many resources to offer to be so disengaged from the affairs of the larger society. Fortunately, there are new ways in which older Americans can remain connected while contributing a lifetime of experience. Organizations such as ReServe help older adults do just that.

Based in New York City, ReServe was created in 2005 to provide meaningful opportunities for older adults to serve their communities and to help transform incoming generations of older Americans into a powerful resource for social change and economic and cultural growth. We do this by matching people who have retired from their primary careers with part-time service-work assignments in the nonprofit and government sectors; this work offers flexibility, social purpose, and a modest stipend.

ReServe works with nonprofits and public institutions to identify the help they need to stay on mission, including such positions as administrative assistants, tutors, financial counselors, marketing managers, writers, or volunteer managers. The agency interviews and selects a candidate who has the relevant skills, experience, and passion to serve. ReServists receive $10 an hour (paid by their employer) and they work 10 to 20 hours a week on ongoing assignments and time-limited projects.

In 2010 ReServists worked a total of 240,000 hours. By the fall of 2011, 430 ReServists were serving at more than 120 different agencies in New York City and Westchester County.

ReServists range in age from 55 to 85. They come from every part of New York City and mirror its demographics with one exception: 70 percent have college degrees. ReServists include retired social workers, office managers, actors, lawyers, sales clerks, teachers, journalists, artists, and researchers, as well as people who have worked at all levels in health care, business, banking, advertising, manufacturing, and government.

One such ReServist is Suwon. She broke race and gender glass ceilings during a 25-year career at Citigroup. By the time she retired in 2006, she was an area investment director and vice president overseeing 28 Citibank financial centers and $4 billion in assets. In 2009 she joined ReServe and was placed in ReServe's READY program, which trained her to help low-income high school juniors and seniors complete their college and financial applications. Suwon has gone above and beyond the call of duty, often working with students and their families after hours. "I left corporate America five years ago with a commitment to do good before I leave this earth," she says. "Helping the students through the [college application] process is a highlight every day." She is in her third year as a READY college coach.

For Sayyid, being a ReServist gives him an opportunity to use his skills to assist others. A ReServist job developer at Queens Library's Job Information Center, he helps job seekers enhance their résumés and perform effective job searches online, and he also provides them with tips on interviewing. Sayyid joined ReServe in 2011 after retiring from his primary career in teaching, which included four years at Tulane University. Sayyid holds an MBA and Ph.D. in history and speaks five languages. The library serves a diverse community, and his language skills are an asset. "Some of the clients who stop by aren't sure how to navigate the job market, especially if they are newly arrived immigrants," he says. "I try to inspire confidence in them. I tell them not to come looking for a job, but instead to look for a career. I want to 'adopt' all of my clients because I want to be in touch with them and see where they are."

Mark is also a READY college coach. As a former immigrant, he can relate well to the students, many of whom are new Americans. Mark escaped from anti-Semitism in Poland in 1969. He has two law degrees, one each from Poland and the United States, and he practiced international and immigration law for more than 30 years. Mark told me that he likes giving back to his community for the personal satisfaction but also to maintain his health. "If you have been working all your life and start doing nothing, your brain and your soul will start to deteriorate," he says. "Structure is good, not just for others but also for your own well-being."

Suwon, Sayyid, and Mark are among hundreds of ReServists who are using their life and career experience to remain healthy and engaged and to make a large impact in their communities.

Everyone has a moral obligation to serve — in some fashion — at any age. We need to activate that moral impulse in those who have retired, and make them feel compelled to serve, to add value to their communities.

33

The Encore Career

by Mark Miller

Mark Miller is a journalist who writes about trends in retirement and aging. He is the author of *The Hard Times Guide to Retirement Security: Practical Strategies for Money, Work and Living*. He writes the syndicated newspaper column "Retire Smart," and also writes retirement columns for *Reuters* and *Morningstar*. Miller blogs at www.RetirementRevised.com. Twitter: @retirerevised.

Career reinvention was a big buzzword among many baby boomers even before the economy crashed in 2008. Surveys showed a large majority of the biggest generation aspired to launch new careers in their 50s and 60s — often in fields where they hoped to make a difference — teaching, health care, or the nonprofit world.

Now, tough new economic realities have transformed career reinvention from a virtue into a necessity for millions of older Americans who aren't ready to retire or simply can't afford to quit working.

But even though times are hard, older boomers refuse to give up their dreams of having second careers with meaning. One person who exemplifies this is Barry Childs, who retired early from Abbott Laboratories at age 55, after a successful corporate career spanning three decades, to launch Africa Bridge, a nonprofit that works to improve economic conditions in villages in Tanzania, and to provide direct support to children there who have been orphaned by the HIV/AIDS crisis.

Childs grew up in Tanzania, where his British father worked as a botanist. He left the country as a teenager in 1969, and in 1998 he returned for the first time to the high mountain villages there. The country was in many ways the same beautiful, peaceful place he remembered from childhood. "What hadn't changed were the people. They were wonderful and welcoming," says Childs. "What had changed was the poverty and HIV/AIDS. The combination was devastating."

Childs decided he had to act. Today, Africa Bridge has trained more than 250 volunteers in 21 communities, providing more than 4,500 children with general, social, and legal services. His organization has helped create 36 income-generating farming cooperatives, and has built classrooms and clinics. Africa Bridge's programs are designed to be self-sustaining, and they give vulnerable village children the possibility of going from eating one meal a day to three. Instead of eating meat three times a year, they have it three times a week.

The transformation of Childs's career — and life — has been profound. It is an example of a trend that is visible in ways large and small across the United States — midlife career reinvention with social purpose. This aspiration is tied to the broader idea that our traditional idea of retirement needs reinvention — a concept that many retirement gurus have struggled to label, so far without much success. In my view, the name that comes closest to defining this trend is: the encore career.

The phrase was coined by Civic Ventures, a California-based nonprofit think tank and incubator for social entrepreneurship led by Marc Freedman, who is among the nation's leading thinkers on how America can redefine the second half of life with a sense of social and individual renewal.

Civic Ventures has launched a movement around encore careers with two main themes: second careers with meaning, and social entrepreneurship. It operates a social networking site (www.encore.org), runs local events all over the country, and also sponsors a high-profile annual award program called the Purpose Prize. The award recognizes older career trailblazers who have demonstrated creative and effective work tackling social problems. It has evolved into a sort of Oscar award for social entrepreneurship, with more than 1,400 nominees each year; five winners receive $100,000 prizes.

At a time when the jobs picture looks bleak, Freedman remains optimistic about the potential contributions of older workers. With people living healthier, longer lives, he argues for creating a new map of life that includes a new stage between the middle years and anything resembling old age.

"As people move into this stage of life, there's a realization that you don't live forever, and that we're a species that passes on from generation to generation," Freedman says. "That's why I think this legacy impulse is so important. It gives us a sense of purpose, a reason to get up in the morning, and use of one's accumulated experience to have an impact in the world and particularly to leave the world a better place than we found it."

Section

HOW WORKING IN RETIREMENT CAN WORK FOR YOU

34

What's Next? Finding Your Dream Job in Retirement

by Kerry Hannon

Kerry Hannon, a career transition, personal finance, and retirement expert, is the author of *What's Next? Follow Your Passion and Find Your Dream Job*, winner of two 2011 Independent Book Publishers medals in the best career/business book categories. She is AARP's jobs expert and their "Great Jobs for Retirees" columnist, as well as a columnist and contributor to *Forbes* magazine, and a nationally acclaimed personal finance contributing editor and retirement correspondent for U.S. *News & World Report*. Hannon is also the author of *Getting Started in Estate Planning, Suddenly Single: Money Skills for Divorcees and Widows, 10 Minute Guide to Retirement for Women*, and *You and Your Money: A Passage from Debt to Prosperity*. Hannon contributes regularly to USA *Today* and SecondAct.com, among other national print and online publications. For more go to www.kerryhannon.com. Twitter:@KerryHannon.

The notion that retirement is all gardening, golfing, and reclining on the beach is out. Meaningful work is in. Yes, some retirees have always taken part-time jobs out of boredom or financial need. What's different now is that baby boomers are approaching work not as a postscript but as a pillar of their "retirement" plans. Even people with healthy retirement savings see earning a half-time income as a safety net.

Work is also what makes it possible to stay healthy, mentally sharp, and engaged, and to squeeze the most juice out of the rest of our lives. It doesn't have to be work in the traditional sense of eight-hour days. I'm talking about flexible schedules, seasonal gigs, and an activity that keeps you alive intellectually, financially, and spiritually. For most of us, a job gives us a sense of purpose, as well as helping us to feel connected and needed.

Here is some practical advice on starting your own retirement career.

1. **Cast a wide net.** Look at your skill set and past experience as transferable to lots of different challenges and fields. You're redirecting or redeploying the skills

you already have in place, not retraining for entirely new ones. Look inside yourself and answer some important questions, such as, *What do I do best?* Ask friends and colleagues too. They might see things that you take for granted.

2. Research. Look for jobs and opportunities that leverage experience. Check out job Web sites like www.encore.org, www.retiredbrains.com, and www.workforce50.com, to get a flavor for what others are doing and what jobs are out there now. Investigate fields like health care, the clergy, elder care, and education, which have a growing demand for workers.

3. Get financially fit. Money is the biggest stumbling block that stops most people from changing fields. For most people, a career restart comes with a financial price tag. It might mean a sizable pay cut to pursue work in a more altruistic field. If you have an entrepreneurial bent, expect start-up costs. You might have expenses such as tuition and loss of medical and retirement benefits, at least for a time. Have a cushion of up to six months of living expenses set aside for transition costs, as well as unexpected emergencies. Pay down debt. Downsize your lifestyle.

4. Boost your credit score. If you need to borrow funds to start your own business, lenders use your credit score to determine whether they should lend you money and what your interest rate will be. If you need to rent office space, landlords may check it to see if you are likely to be a good tenant. And if you're switching to a new company, many employers review it when making the decision to hire. A good score today is 760 and up. You may have some work to do.

5. Keep your hand out of the cookie jar. Don't dip too deep into your core savings. Would-be entrepreneurs aren't necessarily raiding retirement accounts to launch businesses, but they're tapping home equity and other savings, and that has obvious implications for retirement security.

6. Invest in additional education and training. Do your research into the skills or certifications required for your new career. Add the essential skills and degrees before you make the leap. Check out offerings at community colleges for retraining. Consider taking one class at a time. If possible, take some classes while your current employer is still offering tuition reimbursement.

7. Apprentice, volunteer, or moonlight. Do the job first. Volunteering is a great way to get in the door and see what goes on behind the scenes. It's also a networking opportunity. What might sound romantic and wonderful, like running a B&B or a winery, is not so much fun when it becomes your daily routine, requiring long hours and hard work.

8. Focus on smaller companies and nonprofits. They're more likely to value your overall work experience. You can provide the depth of practical knowledge and versatility that's worth two junior hires, and the learning curve is not as steep.

9. Network. In this era of online résumés, it's all about who you know that can get you in the chair for a face-to-face meeting. People want to hire someone who comes with the blessing of an existing employee or colleague. Join Facebook, Twitter, LinkedIn. These are all great ways to pull together your professional network and connect with potential mentors.

10. Ask for help. Find a mentor or two working in your new field. Many corporations provide career coaches and counseling on a limited basis to help employees who have retired or lost their jobs. Check out career centers at your alma mater and those operated by area colleges or local government agencies offering workshops on résumé writing, career counseling, job fairs, and retraining programs. If there's a particular industry you're gunning for, join an association affiliated with it and attend conferences.

11. **Brush up on the latest technology.** Social media platforms such as Facebook, LinkedIn, Twitter, and most recently, Google+ have transformed how you job hunt. You must be comfortable with computers and basic programs, navigating the Web, e-mail, and mobile technology.

12. **Be realistic.** Changing careers doesn't happen on your timetable. And nothing has to be forever. You might have several new careers from here on out. Accept that premise, and it makes a next move more manageable. And who knows? You might do a couple of things at the same time. One 60-year-old woman I know is self-employed as an SAT tutor, a community college associate professor, a personal fitness trainer, and a caterer. Bon appétit!

Note: Portions of this essay originally appeared in Hannon's Forbes.com "Second Verse" column.

35

How to Turn a Hobby into Retirement Income

by Joan Jones

Joan Jones is an award-winning journalist and freelance writer who turned her passion for writing into retirement income by creating blogs and Web sites. Her baby boomer blog is *Tips for Boomer Years* (www.TipsforBoomerYears.com), and her knitting blog is found at Spinning Alpaca Yarns (www.SpinningAlpacaYarns.com).

When you retire, you may need some additional income for extras, or even for necessities. What better way to earn it than by turning a beloved hobby into profit?

Retirement often affords us time to pursue our hobbies. But after you've knitted a dozen scarves, created some woodworking doodads, or converted your beautiful photos into posters, what do you do with all of them? Making your passions profitable might be the next step.

Points to Consider

Once your hobby becomes "work," it may not seem as enjoyable. To do a craft fair, for instance, you need a certain amount of stock. But it's no fun if your wrists and hands begin to hurt, your shoulders ache, and your eyes start burning.

Also, if you are going to rely in any way on the income you make from your hobby, understand that you still have to spend money for supplies, entries into craft fairs, etc., so your profit margin may not be that big initially. If you have a real passion for your hobby, you're likely to spend even more. However, should you create a business and make a profit, you can deduct supplies on your taxes.

If you're still sure you want to turn your hobby into an income-producing business, here are some steps to take.

Start by Assessing

1. **What is your skill level?** Can you produce items quickly and in quantity, and make your product look professional?

2. **How much time do you want to devote?** Making

enough items for a craft fair, for instance, is very time-consuming, as is creating a Web site or online store.

Marketing Your Product

1. **Find a niche market.** Rather than trying to be all things to all people, it's easier to make a profit if you specifically cater to one niche or group of people. Take knitting, for instance. You could create your pieces from organic yarn, make only baby clothes or blankets, specialize in prayer shawls, or knit only with hand-painted, hand-dyed yarns.

It's easy for me to give knitting examples because that's what I love doing, but if you are a photographer you could specialize in nature photography, scenery, animals, cute puppies, whatever. If you do woodworking, focus on wooden toys or fancy shelves. If you make candles, use only soy or natural fragrances.

2. **Research your market.** Who is your competition, and how do they manage their business? Visit some craft fairs and see if you can spot a niche that needs to be filled, or one that is popular but has less competition. Talk to others who are doing what you want to do — crafters are generally very nice and helpful people.

3. Decide *how* you will sell your product. Are you willing and able to spend your weekends holding down the fort at your craft fair table? Could you travel to distant craft fairs? You can also sell through Web sites that feature only handcrafted items, like Etsy.com or Artfire.com, where setting up an online store is free, and they take just a small percentage of the amount of your sale. Remember that online customers usually pay through PayPal, which also takes a small percentage of each transaction, so price accordingly.

4. Once you determine your product and your selling method, consider your financial goals. **How much money would you like to make?** Just enough to pay for your own materials? Enough to pay for one of the household bills, or to give you some cash for that extra trip? It's important to know the scope and purpose of your hobby business.

Other Ways to Profit from Your Hobby

1. Write about your hobby. Even if you don't make products, you can still profit from your hobby. One way is to create a blog or Web site where you can place some affiliate ads. You can review books or products, and, if giving a good recommendation, sell it via the

Amazon.com affiliate program or a Google AdSense account, or find your own companies to represent.

Many programs and books explain how to create a for-profit blog. This requires a little computer expertise, but again, there are many low-cost programs to help you. To maintain a self-hosted WordPress blog, expect to spend about $100 a year. You can also start with a free blogging platform, such as Blogger.com or TypePad.

2. Write an e-book about your hobby. If you've been doing your hobby for a while, or you're in a popular niche, you probably have a lot of expertise in that area. Consider writing an e-book that will help readers develop a passion for your hobby. Again, there are books and programs to help you create and market an e-book.

Amazon now offers an easy-to-use platform for selling e-books to Kindle owners, or you could sell through ClickBank.com, which allows affiliates to sell your e-book for you, and then you split the profit with them.

3. Teach classes. If you like interacting with others and sharing your hobby, contact your local craft or hobby store, senior center, or community college. Find out if they need an instructor, or if there is a special hobby technique that they don't currently teach.

You can also create podcasts and teach online. Again, there are many books and programs to explain this process.

Resources for Starting a Craft Business

Go to Etsy.com or Artfire.com and click on "How to Create a Store."

Search on Amazon.com or check your local bookstore for books on "turning a craft into a profit."

If you hope to turn your hobby into retirement income, realize that you'll have to work to make it successful. However, spending your days focusing on your passion makes it unlike any other "job." You'll have fun and probably make a lot of new friends along the way.

36

Starting a Home-Based Business in Retirement

by Art Koff

Art Koff is the founder of RetiredBrains.com and the author of the reference guide, *Invent Your Retirement: Resources for the Good Life*. He speaks regularly on the challenges being faced by older Americans and has been interviewed as an authority on national TV and in major publications.

Many older Americans have found they are unable to retire and live anywhere near the lifestyle they anticipated as they planned for their retirement years. The value of their retirement plans, savings, homes, pensions, etc. have all substantially diminished, and they have discovered unexpected expenses they did not anticipate.

More and older Americans are forced to work longer to help make ends meet. A 2011 ERBI survey reveals that 74 percent of Americans say they plan to work in retirement to supplement their savings. In this economy, for some older Americans who are out of work, it is sometimes better to spend the majority of effort looking for a "work from home job" or a small business enterprise to begin than to spend a lot of time and effort in a fruitless job search.

In speaking with those who have contacted me via my RetiredBrains.com Web site, many say they have at least temporarily given up seeking a full-time job and are now searching for other ways to make some money. When asked how they went about this search, we were told things like, "I reviewed my abilities, interests, resources, skills, hobbies, etc. and used this information to start my research."

5 Ideas for Starting a Home-Based Business

1. Use your background and strengths to freelance your expertise to thousands of companies who are now hiring on this basis. Register on the many sites that provide freelancers with job opportunities and search these sites for work. Check http://retiredbrains. com/Home/Work+From+Home/Freelancing/default. aspx for a list of sites.

2. Consider selling for the many direct sales firms like Mary Kay, Silpada, Pampered Chef, Avon, Tupperware, etc. In most cases companies that involve direct selling require you to purchase some product for you to sell, but the "starter kit" of training materials is generally not very expensive. For a list of direct selling companies with links back to each, check out http://retiredbrains. com/Home/Work+From+Home/Direct+Selling/default. aspx.

3. Sell or resell online. Many people start out by selling items from around their homes but later they purchase items and resell them at a profit. If you have items to sell online but you're not sure which site to use — eBay, craigslist, or Amazon.com — check out http://retiredbrains.com/Home/Work+From+Home/ Selling+On-Line/default.aspx to see a list of products along with sites best suited for their sale. Some entrepreneurs also sell the products they purchase at flea markets, craft fairs, and farmer's markets.

4. Start a small business. See if any of the following examples might be right for you: a landscaping/ gardening business, perhaps including grass cutting and snow removal; a small painting and house

repair business; a dog walking and pet-sitting business; a business cleaning and organizing closets and garages (see http://retiredbrains.com/Home/Start+Your+Own+Business/default.aspx for examples of people who have done this).

5. Purchase a franchise you can operate out of your home. These kinds of businesses vary substantially and include everything from dog walking/training to babysitting to cleaning services and tax preparation services and even medical billing and tutoring. All usually require less of an investment than franchises that are tied to a location where rent must be paid, like restaurants, offices, or retail stores. As franchises, however, they do provide the benefits of getting help from a company headquarters as well as a set of proven rules and procedures to follow for a successful business. For a list, check out http://retiredbrains.com/Home/Start+Your+Own+Business/Franchise+List/default.aspx where you will find franchises like Rent-A-Grandma, Guard Now (security guard service, janitorial agency), New Pro Publication Golf Business, Novus Glass (automotive glass company), Paint Bull, Pajama Man School (home-based insurance), Tire Inflation Maintenance, Vernon

Street Capital (financial services), Coupon Starter, Pet Corner, and many more.

Obviously, starting a home-based business is easier since the advent of the Internet. Entrepreneurs can use craigslist to advertise, and to find clients and purchasers for products and services, etc.; they can use eBay to buy products and in some cases to sell them; they can build relationships on Facebook, LinkedIn, etc.; they can create a home page to market their enterprise. Check RetiredBrains for a complete list of what you'll need to open a home-based office: http://retiredbrains.com/Home/Start+Your+Own+Business/Open+Your+Home+Office/default.aspx.

According to market research, there were around 12 million full-time, home-based freelancers and independent contractors in America at the end of 2010. It's estimated that number will jump to 14 million by 2015. The Bureau of Labor Statistics reports that between 2008 and January 2011, the number of self-employed older Americans rose by 5 percent among 55- to 64-year-olds, and the number of entrepreneurs over the age of 65 increased by 29 percent. So you see, you'll be in good company — and you may just find the kind of fulfilling business that will make your retirement enjoyable — and profitable.

37

Six Ways to Get Paid to Travel During Retirement

by Nancy Collamer, M.S.

Nancy Collamer, M.S., is a career coach, speaker, and author of the upcoming *Second-Act Careers: 50+ Ways to Profit from Your Passions During Semi-Retirement*. She is one of the country's leading experts on lifestyle-friendly careers and her advice has been featured in numerous media outlets including NBC *Nightly News*, the *New York Times*, CNN, *Redbook*, MORE, O, *The Oprah Magazine*, and *Fortune*. Based in Old Greenwich, Connecticut, Collamer works with clients around the country by telephone. She holds an M.S. in career development from the College of New Rochelle and a B.A. in psychology from UNC/Chapel Hill. She can be contacted through her Web site at www.mylifestylecareer.com.

How would you like to actually get paid to travel during your retirement? Thanks to the Internet and the global economy, there are now more options than ever for earning an income while traveling in the United States or overseas. If your retirement plans include dreams of spending time in cool places, read on to learn six fun ways you can earn while enjoying life on the road:

1. Train to be a tour director. Tour directors are hired by tour operators to lead groups of people on multiday excursions in different locations throughout the world. As a tour director, you'll be responsible for keeping your charges entertained, engaged, safe, and on schedule while you travel from site to site. According to Frank Slater, president of the International Guide Academy, tour directors earn an average of about $3,000 over the course of a ten-day assignment, in addition to receiving compensation for all costs associated with their travel. This is a job with tremendous growth potential; more than 80 million Americans travel on group tours annually, and with the baby boomers entering retirement, those numbers are likely to increase over the next decade.

Helpful resource: International Guide Academy (www. bepaidtotravel.com).

2. Work as a part-time tour guide. If the thought of globe-trotting for a living as a tour director has you worried about spending too much time on the road, you might prefer working as a tour guide in your own city and state. The variety of tours being offered is growing all the time: you can lead food tours, ghost tours, tours that cater to grandparents, and tours unique to a specific locale or historic site. Most guides are able to work on a part-time basis, earning $20 to $50 per hour (bilingual guides can command up to $75 per hour).

Helpful resource: You can earn a Certified Tour Professional certification through the National Tour Association (www.ntaonline.com).

3. Work as an interim innsitter. If you've ever dreamed about running your own bed-and-breakfast, but worry about the headaches involved with owning an inn, consider getting trained to work as an innsitter instead. As the name implies, innsitters provide temporary relief for innkeepers who need to get away for a few days; it's the equivalent of being a Mary Poppins for the bed-and-breakfast set. Innsitters can work at different properties around the country and overseas. Most innsitters work on a part-time basis, traveling to assignments as their schedule and lifestyle permits.

Helpful resource: Professional Association of Innkeepers International (www.innkeeping.org).

4. **Work and live in the national parks:** How would you like an opportunity to live and work inside the splendor of our national parks? If you want to experience our parks as more than just a mere tourist, you'll be pleased to know that the parks hire people for a wide variety of jobs, including botanists, gift shop sales, administrative posts, maintenance workers, and oral interpreters. Most positions are seasonal and, in addition to paying a salary, many parks offer their employees access to subsidized housing and meals.

Helpful resource: Consult the parks' official Web site at www.nps.gov to search job listings.

5. **Teach English overseas.** Even in a weak global economy, the opportunities to teach English overseas are robust. In most instances, all you need to qualify for a teaching job is a bachelor's degree, but candidates with either advanced training or a degree in teaching English as a second language (TESOL) have access to greater job opportunities and earnings potential. Your compensation can range from a small living stipend

to salaries of $50,000 or more, depending on your expertise, experience, and location.

Helpful resource: TransitionsAbroad.com (www. transitionsabroad.com) has listings for teaching jobs, as well as other listings of overseas employment.

6. **Do house sitting/property caretaking.** Can you imagine getting paid to live in a beautiful chateau or estate in an exotic location? It's not a fantasy. In exchange for providing services as a house sitter or property caretaker, you can live rent-free in accommodations that include ranches, castles, estates, and farms. In addition to enjoying free rent, your compensation might include a work stipend, meals, or travel expenses.

Helpful resource: Caretakers Gazette (www. caretakersgazette.com) is an excellent site for finding information and listings of opportunities.

Intrigued? I hope you'll take the time to explore the resources provided to learn more about the many exciting opportunities for blending travel, income, and adventure. And no matter which option you choose to pursue, I wish you safe travels and happy trails!

Section

5

A NEW FREEDOM
TO BE YOURSELF

38

Why You Need to Know 'What Color Is Your Parachute? for Retirement'

by John E. Nelson

John Nelson is coauthor of *What Color is Your Parachute? for Retirement*. His work has been covered in the *New York Times*, *Wall Street Journal*, *USA Today*, and elsewhere. Nelson has led workshops for the federal government, the United Way, AARP, college alumni associations, and Fortune "100 Best Companies" employers. His Web site is www.johnenelson.com.

W hat's the retirement stage of life about, anyway?

Of course, we all have a mental list of things we'd like to do, once we retire. But there's a strange truth about that list. Rather than focusing on what we truly desire in retirement, it's often driven by what we don't like about our working life. For example, if our job has us feeling worn out (or burned out), we imagine just taking it easy for a while. If we feel like we didn't have enough vacation time, we imagine traveling, or taking longer trips. If we feel like our weekends were too short, we imagine doing more household projects. If we feel like we didn't have enough time for family and friends, we put them first on our list for retirement. It's a strange, but natural, way to approach retirement. Once we recognize what we've been missing out on, we vow to get more of it in retirement. But even though this approach is natural — it's not enough.

Rather than being driven by what you've been missing, it's more powerful to intentionally identify all the elements you truly desire, which will support your well-being. The book I coauthored with Richard Nelson Bolles, *What Color Is Your Parachute? for Retirement* (now in its second edition), helps you do that. Specific tools show you how to create the big picture — including choosing where to live, making your money last, finding your unique way of staying healthy, building circles of social support, and living by your deepest values. Once you have that larger perspective, it becomes obvious that retirement has a higher purpose — it's really about finding your life's work.

But in this case, the word "work" probably doesn't have anything to do with a job (although it might). Rather, your life's work is about finding the reason that you're still here, on Earth. Your life's work is about discovering and pursuing a set of experiences, or accomplishments, or insights that are unique to you. Your life's work is about bringing out the best in yourself and in those around you.

It may seem weird, but in some ways your life now is similar to when you were first starting your career. At that stage, you wanted to find something that was fun, that you knew you could do well, and that you would be proud of. At that time, it was about having a paycheck. Now, it's about having a sense of fulfillment. But the process you use is essentially the same. How do you find your life's work in retirement?

First, you'll want to reconnect with your strongest interests. What subjects out in the world fascinate you so completely that you love to keep learning about them, talking about them, and dreaming about them? In the beginning of your career, if you were lucky, your work was related to your fields of fascination. But over the years, your job changed, and you became less fascinated. Or maybe you never really discovered your strongest interests. Or you knew what your interests were, but you never found an interesting job. Whatever happened along the way, now is the ideal time to find your fascinations again, out there in the world.

Second, you'll want to remember your greatest skills. What do you do best? What are the talents and abilities that you absolutely love to use? These aren't the specific skills that your job demanded — but the deeper ones that you bring to all of life's situations. These are your transferable skills, which you'll want to transfer to your next stage of life. They're not as obvious as your fascinations, because they're inside of you instead of out in the world. But when you think about the times that you were really engaged and energized by your work, you were probably using your talents. On the other hand, if you weren't engaged in your job, and you haven't used your greatest skills for years, it's even more important to remember them now. After all, instead of using them for your job, now you can use them for yourself and for those you love.

Third, you'll want to clarify your deepest values in life. What gives you a sense of meaning? When you were getting established in your career, or providing for your family, or caring for your children, having a sense of purpose was automatic. You didn't need to think about it. But in retirement, if your only purpose in life is to entertain yourself — will that be enough? At first, retirement can seem like one long vacation, and the whole point is simply to have fun. But then after weeks, or months, or years, you may begin to yearn for . . . something more. You may want to be of service to something outside of yourself — something that represents your highest values. And, lucky for you, you'll have the time and energy to devote to that higher purpose.

It's worthwhile to do the work of rediscovering your interests, skills, and values, because any one of them can become a powerful force in your life. Any one of them, alone, can help you create the retirement of your dreams. But when you combine all three, you have a trifecta! So, on one piece of paper begin making a list of all your interests, skills, and values. When you see all of them together, you'll start making connections and prioritizing them. As you start imagining new opportunities, you'll think of people to involve. Before you know it, you'll actually begin moving closer to what you've written down. You'll be on the path to your life's work!

By the way, once you've written down your interests, skills, and values on that one piece of paper, you might use it in other ways, too. Beyond helping you find your life's work, it may be the beginning of finding a meaningful job, if necessary. Heaven forbid!

39

Don't Let It Take a Crisis

by Jack Phelps, ChFC

Jack Phelps, ChFC, is the *Relaxing* Retirement Coach and the creator of the *Relaxing* Retirement Coaching Program™. Developed over the last 17 years, the program provides the "missing structure" that individuals and couples need to make a seamless and relaxing transition to their retirement years so they can confidently do everything they want to do without worrying about money. Phelps publishes *The Retirement Coach "Strategy of the Week"* e-mail series, available from www.TheRetirementCoach.com.

During a recent two-week stretch, I received several pieces of unfortunate news.

I learned that one of my *Relaxing* Retirement Coaching Program™ members was diagnosed with leukemia. Another member developed a degenerative nerve condition, causing him to suddenly lose a good portion of his eyesight. After five years in remission, one of my other program members started up a whole new round of chemotherapy. And I learned that after retiring last year, another member's rapidly progressing Alzheimer's now prohibits him from being left alone.

Wake-up Call

The convergence of all this bad news provided me with one of my life's "wake-up calls." We've all heard the phrase, "Don't wait for a crisis in your life to motivate you to prioritize and do what you *really* want to do." It would be great if it didn't take a crisis to get us to *think* and *prioritize* differently.

For me, one of those crisis events occurred when I was 20 years old, when my mother got sick and passed away at the very young age of 57. After dealing with the reality of losing my mother (unfortunately, she was terminally ill for 19 months), the lesson for me was: *Never wait to do anything, because you never know when it can all be taken away from you.*

I would certainly have preferred that it didn't take losing my mother for me to learn that lesson about prioritizing better.

Progressing Toward Something

One of the great advantages of retirement is that you are free of the pressures you had to face at work. However, without the deadlines and structure that work provides, some people feel lost. That's why it's so important, whether or not you're still working, to give significant thought to what you want most out of life and then get busy doing it.

As you objectively look around at all the people you know, something becomes obvious: certain individuals are more successful and happy than others. Not only that, but in stark contrast to most people whose optimism fades with age, these same individuals are more energetic, enthusiastic, and confident.

There are many explanations for this, but the number-one reason for a loss of momentum in retirement is a lack of prioritizing and goal setting. Without it, everyone loses their sense of direction and confidence.

Instead of being excited about what lies ahead, retirees become increasingly nostalgic about their youthful years and the "good old days." However, those who continuously clarify and act on their goals benefit from the law of *compound interest*; i.e., as with money, the more you invest in visualizing and working toward a better future, the better your future automatically becomes.

The most exciting part of life is knowing that you're

progressing toward something. That's why it's so important to have written goals in retirement, not just weakly stated ones like New Year's resolutions that quickly turn sour.

My Recommendation to You

At least once every six months, take a moment to step back and think with no distractions.

Clarify and prioritize what's most important to you — don't wait for a crisis to motivate you to do so.

Lock the doors, turn off the television, shut off the cell phone and the ringer on your phone, pull out a pad of paper and a pen, and sit in a comfortable chair in your favorite spot in your home. Tell everyone to give you some "quiet" time. While you're in that spot, relax and think ahead 20 years from now, 10 years from now, or even just 3 years from now.

Put yourself out there and look back to today. Looking back over those years:

- *What* would you like to say you did?
- *Who* did you spend your time with?
- *Where* did you spend your time?

Once you've compiled your list, arrange it in order of

importance to you personally.

Ask yourself, "What steps do I have to take right now to make this happen?"

And, "Who might be able to help me?"

Keep the list visible to you, so you see it on a daily basis.

Share your list with people who are close to you. Don't waste your time sharing it with those who don't truly have your best interests and happiness at heart. You will be amazed at how much everyone wants to help you get what you want when you ask for help.

Your retirement years provide you with a new lease on life. You now have the opportunity to clean the slate and spend all of your time doing *what you want, when you want, where you want,* and *with* whomever you choose. However, that doesn't just fall into place without careful thought and action. To get what you really want, you have to plan and act constantly.

Life can be short. Don't wait for a crisis to realize this.

Get out there and soak it all up. Be busy! Be exhausted!

40

Doing 60

by Gloria Steinem

Gloria Steinem is a writer, feminist, and social reformer. After graduating from Smith College, she went to New York City as a freelance writer, first attracting attention with her article, "I Was a Playboy Bunny," an exposé based on her own undercover work in a New York City Playboy Club. Among her many lifetime achievements, Steinem is the founder and original publisher of Ms. magazine.

Age is supposed to create more serenity, calm, and detachment from the world, right? Well, I'm finding just the reverse. The older I get, the more intensely I feel about the world around me, including things I once thought too small for concern; the more connected I feel to nature, though I used to prefer human invention; the more poignancy I find not only in very old people, who always got to me, but also in children; the more likely I am to feel rage when people are rendered invisible, and also to claim my own place; the more I can risk saying "no" even if "yes" means approval; and most of all, the more able I am to use my own voice, to know what I feel, and to say what I think; in short, to *express* without also having to *persuade.*

Some of this journey's content is uniquely mine, and I find excitement in its solitary, edge-of-the-world sensation of entering new territory with the wind whistling past my ears. Who would have imagined, for instance, that I, once among the most externalized of people, would now think of meditation as a tool of revolution (without self-authority, how can we keep standing up to external authority)? or consider inner space more important to explore than outer space? or dismay even some feminists by saying that power is also internal? or voice thoughts as contrary to everything I read in the newspapers as: The only lasting arms control is how we raise our children?

On the other hand, I know my journey's form is a common one. I'm exploring the other half of the circle — something that is especially hard in this either/or culture that tries to make us into one thing for life, and treats change as if it were a rejection of the past.

Nonetheless, I see more and more people going on to a future that builds on the past but is very different from it. I see many women who spent the central years of their lives in solitary creative work or nurturing husbands and children — and some men whose work or temperament turned them inward too — who are discovering the external world of activism, politics, and tangible causes with all the same excitement that I find in understanding less tangible ones. I see many men who spent most of their lives working for external rewards, often missing their own growth as well as their children's, who are now nurturing second families, their internal lives, or both — and a few women who are following this pattern too, because they needed to do the unexpected before they could feel less than trapped by the expected.

I'm also finding a new perspective that comes from leaving the central plateau of life, and seeing more clearly the tyrannies of social expectation I've left behind. For women especially — and for men too, if they've been limited to stereotypes — we've traveled past the point when society cares very much about who we are or what we do. Most of our social value ended at 50 or so, when our youth-related powers of sexuality, childbearing, and hard work came to an end — at least, by the standards of a culture that assigns such roles — and the few powerful positions reserved for the old and wise are rarely ours anyway. Though the growing neglect and invisibility may shock and grieve us greatly at first and feel like "a period of free fall," to use Germaine Greer's phrase, it also creates a new freedom to be ourselves — without explanation. As Greer concludes in *The Change*, her book about women and aging: "The climacteric marks the end of apologizing. The chrysalis of conditioning has once and for all to break and the female woman finally to emerge."

From this new vantage point, I see that my notion of age bringing detachment was probably just one more bias designed to move some groups out of the way. If so, it's even more self-defeating than most biases — and on a much grander scale — for sooner or later, this one will catch up with all of us. Yet we've allowed a youth-centered culture to leave us so estranged from our future selves that, when asked about the years beyond 50, 60, or 70 — all part of the average human life span, providing we can escape hunger, violence, and other epidemics — many people can see only a blank screen, or one on which they project fear of disease and dependency. This incomplete social map makes the last third of life an unknown country and leaves men stranded after their work lives are over, but it ends so much earlier for women that only a wave of noisy feminists has made us aware of its limits by going public with experiences that were once beyond its edge, from menopause as a rite of passage into what Margaret Mead called "postmenopausal zest," to the news that raised life expectancies and lowered birth rates are making older people, especially older women, a bigger share of many nations, from Europe to Japan, than ever before in history. I hope to live to the year 2030, and see what this country will be like when one in four women is 65 or over — as is one in five of the whole population. Perhaps we will be perennial flowers who "re-pot" ourselves and bloom in many times.

41

Turning 65: Minding Your Ps and Qs and Rs

by Rick Kimball

Richard S. (Rick) Kimball is a Maine-based freelance writer and photographer. He and his wife, Tirrell, own and operate Green Timber Publications, a small press producing religious education curricula for use in Unitarian Universalist congregations. Kimball began his writing and editing career as a reporter, columnist, and city editor at what was then the Guy Gannett newspapers of Portland, Maine. He next became a full-time writer and editor for J. Weston Walch, Publisher, producing supplementary educational materials for secondary schools. He has written religious education material for the national Unitarian Universalist Association, and in the areas of creativity, local history, and human sexuality. He holds a bachelor's degree from Harvard College, and a master's from Columbia University Graduate School of Journalism.

W hen we're young, birthdays are about getting things — like cards, cakes, toys, clothes if times are tough, and maybe friendly spanks with one to grow on. Later birthdays are about getting rid of things — like jobs when we turn 65.

Birthday expectations turn around, as does much else in life. A good thing, too. Turning around can mean turning out right, because our lives are backward now.

We begin in full dependence, penniless and unadorned. We move through infancy and early childhood under tightening constraint, into schools where we encounter additional controls. Inner resources are already ours, but, innocent and inexperienced, we do not yet know what they are. When we try a surging strength that seems beyond the norm, our controls may stomp it out.

We do not find ourselves; we find what others want. I became a childhood ace at following to a fault. When a teacher announced that the brightest kids have the worst handwriting, I destroyed my own. Years later, a college professor would return a handwritten exam and send me to my room to type it.

We need a grand transposition. As soon as we can walk and talk, the state should hand us each a pile of cash and set us free to find our way. We then could feed our senses through our youth, and grow serious later on. Becoming good at what we loved would win us work and earn enough to carry us into neo-infancy, a stage to lose those jobs along with thoughts and lives, without the need for Alzheimer's to help.

Maybe someday the world really will get things right and turn itself around. But people reaching 65 today must move on without the relief of system reversal. We can turn only our own lives around.

The movie *Beginners* speaks to all this. After his wife of 44 years dies, the 75-year-old lead declares himself gay and throws himself into a passionate affair with a younger man. Had he lived his life backward, he could have escaped the controls of heterosexual expectation and marriage. He could have found himself much earlier.

Fortunately for you with decades of practice at accepting rules, there are two good rules to follow at your 65th. The first is to notice where you are — two-thirds of the way through life, assuming you will live to be 95-plus. There's the true meaning of 65: Hey, our time comes now or not at all.

The second rule is to use that time well by minding the P's and Q's and R's of becoming 65, and do it backwards, in the spirit of turning things around.

Begin with the R's: Review and Reflection — not **Retirement.** Whether to retire is a secondary decision. Review your life and reflect on it. How do you wish to use your remaining years? Decide on that and do it. I did not stop work when I turned 65. I chose to rid myself of something else instead. I gave up embarrassment over minor matters, like absentmindedly wearing unmatched shoes, something I had done a short time before, to the great amusement of a friend.

With some unplanned and sporadic review and reflection, I opted to continue my freelance career, focusing more tightly on my interests of writing and photography, interests I had first recognized in my 20s. Had I lived my life backward, I could have discovered them more easily, without the angst of needing a career when I had too little experience to know what it should be. Now I do know, and I won't give it up until a much later birthday.

Move on to the Q's: Quiet and Quirky. Take some quiet time for more review and reflection. This will help you feel your way around all the "I can't because's" that come to mind as you think about focusing on what you truly wish to be and do. The process will help you move on to renewal. And the quirky? That's the core that's truly you, the idiosyncratic self, a force that now deserves a time to fly.

Which brings us to the P's: Personal and Positive. Be personal. Dig into yourself as you review and reflect, dig in and don't let go. No, it won't hurt, at least for very long. That's the positive truth. And if being positive sounds like a tired cliché, think backward and forget you have ever heard the idea before. Be positive. What's to lose? Who'll do it for you?

I passed my own 65th a few years ago, and the rules have worked well for me. I now know the essentials I must carry forth toward the end: writing, photography, humor, spirituality, and love. I recognized only one of these at age 18, when I was supposed to be sorting out my life. I saw only the humor.

Those essentials give me focus and strength and even some pride as I move into my increasingly dicey final years, but accepting my core did not come all at once or easily. Illness proved a turning point. I suffered two night seizures in my late 60s, out of the dark and into the dark, from nowhere to nowhere. My wife heard me breathing strangely in the predawn, and could not wake me. Fearing a stroke, she called 911. "You are epileptic," the neurologist announced. The term frightens me still, but I see the positive side. The seizures felt like practice for death. They said I might not get my full final third. They said to focus on who I was and how to spend the rest of whatever I did get.

I emerged from the void of the first seizure in an emergency room, frightened and lost, not knowing where I was, who I was, what I was. Slowly my core reappeared, humor first. When a medic asked, "What is your name?" I did not know, so I responded instead with a joke. Struggling through the haze, I found that the me was already there, and my audience was waiting with smiles.

Medicine seems to control the seizures. I can reasonably hope never to have another. But if hope fails, I plan to say this as reality returns: "Wow, what an orgasm that was!" I will not let the caregivers coddle me. I will make them envy me instead.

Two rules, two R's, two Q's, two P's. May these pairs work for you at 65, as they still seem to work for me.

Happy 65th, with one to grow on, an extra rule: Rid yourself of the need to take yourself (or me) too seriously. Think winter sledding, and enjoy the ride down.

42

Lessons from Grief

by Joan Price

Joan Price (www.joanprice.com) calls herself an "advocate for ageless sexuality." She is the author of *Naked at Our Age: Talking Out Loud about Senior Sex*, *Better Than I Ever Expected: Straight Talk about Sex After Sixty*, and several books about health and fitness. Price also speaks professionally about senior sex and about fitness. Visit her award-winning blog about sex and aging at www.nakedatourage.com. Price lives in Sebastopol, California, where she teaches contemporary line dancing — which she calls "the most fun you can have with both feet on the floor."

My driven, fast-paced routine was an asset for a professional writer, even a virtue — or so I told myself. Editors could count on me: I never missed a deadline, always gave more than expected, was committed to excellence. I was fueled by the adrenaline rush of having just enough time for my projects, but never extra days or even hours. I thrived on sleep deprivation.

My never-miss-a-deadline, crowning glory occurred one storm-filled winter when I was under a tight deadline for a magazine article. I was scheduled for an in-person interview in another city on a day when many of the roads of my rural, Northern California town were flooded. I had anticipated the water rising by staying overnight with a friend in a slightly less vulnerable part of town and parking my car on a hill within walking distance. As the storm progressed, although my car was safely above the flood line, I couldn't get to it because the water in one section of the walking route was up to my hips.

Cancel the interview? Never! My friend's husband, tall enough to wade through the water, pulled me in a rowboat to dry land, and I got in the car and to the interview on schedule, submitting my article on time. A perfect record, despite high water.

Now I look back and shake my head. Why didn't I just cancel the darned interview? What was so important that I couldn't spend the morning helping my friend move furniture and art supplies from her flooded art studio, rather than rushing off to do a magazine interview? Where were my values?

But I didn't learn this lesson for a few more decades. I didn't learn it until my husband was dying of cancer. Robert was the love of my life, whom I met when I was 57 and he was 64. Our love affair was so exhilarating and profound that I switched writing topics from health and fitness to senior sex, celebrating our love by writing *Better Than I Ever Expected: Straight Talk About Sex After Sixty.*

In April 2008, less than seven years after our first kiss and not quite two years into our marriage, we knew that Robert's cancer treatments weren't working, and we wouldn't have much more time. Not that any couple knows how much time they have left, but for us, the only deadline that mattered gave us no more than a few months.

I wrote to editors that I couldn't accept assignments and cancelled those I already had. I put the book idea I was developing on hold.

I have no regrets about how I changed my life those last months of his life. How easy it was, compared to the rest of what we were facing, to drop out of deadlines — in fact, to drop out of the frenzy that had driven my entire life to that point. I didn't want to look back on this time and say, "I couldn't spend Robert's last months with him because I was on deadline for a magazine article."

Only Robert mattered, and spending the last of our time together.

After Robert died, I went into profound grief and depression. I couldn't, wouldn't work. Instead of churning out clever and informative articles from my ergonomic computer chair, I sat in the living room, crying and handwriting in my journal. I had set aside journaling 30 years earlier when I started writing professionally and needed the speed and efficiency of my thoughts streaming directly from my brain to the screen. Now, writing longhand created a slow, meandering journey from my heart to my tear-spotted pages. I relished the slowing down.

During my grief time, I also read novels. I've always loved reading fiction, but that was another activity I had ceased to make time for, with so many books demanding my attention for my work. Now, I could read for hours with no goal other than to immerse myself in another writer's world. Every few pages, I'd look out the window to see new roses blooming, or birds swooping and tittering, or an intricate spider-web glistening with raindrops. Robert, an artist, had taught me to stop and really look at nature. I took each new sight as a gift from him.

As I read, contemplated, watched, and wrote, I remember thinking with startling clarity, "I would really enjoy this kind of life — if I weren't so miserable!"

I decided then that when I found my way back to an active and joyful life, I would make time for reading, journaling, and seeing. I would hold onto the gifts that only a slowed-down life can give us, because we can't notice what we have if we're rushing to the next thing.

We humans are remarkably resilient. Eventually, one day of healing at a time, I returned to living productively, laughing, enjoying my life. But I never returned to the hectic pace that used to define me, and I never will.

I'm about to turn 68 as I write this, and although I love my work too much to retire fully, I have slowed down immensely. I've read more novels in the past year than in the three decades before that. I don't write for magazines anymore, though a good book project or blog topic gets my enthusiastic attention. I make time for friends who barely saw me when I was buried under deadlines, and I've made new friends. What I would have seen as self-indulgent a few years ago now feels self-nurturing.

Many of our generation can't retire, or choose not to, but we still have slow-down lessons we can apply to our lives so that we live full, rich, emotional lives. As I pursue what I call "semiretirement" — though it seems like a fuller time, not a "semi" anything — I try to follow my own advice:

- Do what matters day by day, hour by hour.

- Follow my passions.

- Stay healthy by enjoying physical activity every day — and plenty of it.

- Nourish my mind with intellectual activity.

- Make time for pleasure reading.

- Accept only work that feels important.

- Show the people in my life that I appreciate and love them. Be there for them.

- Be grateful every minute for the love I've had the honor of receiving — and giving.

43

"Doing" Resilience: A Virtual Ritual of Transformation

by Carol Orsborn, Ph.D.

Dr. Carol Orsborn is the author of 20 books, including the forthcoming *Fierce with Age: Confessions of a Smart, Spiritual Woman Who Turned Sixty and Forgot Everything* and *The Art of Resilience*. She is CEO of the Fierce with Age Center for Spiritual Aging and executive director of CoroFaith, providing audio-based spiritual content to the aging-in-place community. Formerly senior strategist with VibrantNation.com, Orsborn is an internationally respected thought leader on spirituality and aging and on motivating boomer women at the deepest levels. She received her doctorate from Vanderbilt University, specializing in religion and adult development. She has spoken on such topics as "Resilience 2.0" (ResiliencePartners.net) for such clients as the Walt Disney Company, ABC, Wellpoint, and Ford. Consulting clients include Humana's RealforMe.com.

Once upon a time, resilience was thought to be something one could acquire with sheer grit and determination. When our strategies didn't work, we were taught to fall back upon the kind of stoicism captured in the saying, "Don't cry over spilled milk." Back then, there was a simplicity and a logic to everything from economic prosperity to conventional warfare, which inspired us to believe that we could alleviate any potential source of stress simply by working smarter, harder, and longer.

VUCA Times

Welcome to a new era. There is nothing simple nor logical about the times in which we now live, and our beliefs about what it takes to recover from change and challenge have taken a hit as well. In fact, it was none other than the United States military who came up with the best description of our times. They coined the phrase "VUCA" as an acronym for "volatile, uncertain, complex, and ambiguous." Just as the military has had to adapt to new threats and strategies, so must we learn how to operate in a world in which uncertainty is a way of life. While we should always do what we can to alter our circumstances, bringing as much external mastery into our lives as possible, never has it been more important to tap internal resources, such as intuition, expanded perspective, and discernment — and to open ourselves to divine guidance as well.

Whether you have had a spiritual practice upon which you've relied for decades — or are brand-new to wanting to explore the quieter spectrum of the full human potential — it is a gift to now have the time to create the environment that will help you develop a more resilient outlook.

What Is a Ritual?

In the academic discipline from which I hail, History and Critical Theory of Religion, we call this special time "ritual." Rituals, we learn, are the container for created sacred space. For some of us, going to religious services serves this purpose. For others, it may be visiting a museum and sitting quietly before an inspiring painting or taking your flute to a favorite place in nature and serenading the trees.

I find the endless variations of ritual, the creativity that is brought to the occasion, and the profound inner changes that can occur, endlessly fascinating. Many of you are already familiar with elements that can be assembled to comprise your own personal ritual. For instance, sitting in silence, lighting candles, and the like. What turns these into a ritual is adding the elements of intentionality and repetition. In other words, you set aside a predetermined period of time, with a particular intention, and make a commitment to repeat the elements you've selected on a regular basis. There's room for experimentation and inspiration, of course, and it's worth reviewing both tried-and-true and new ritual elements that have the power to help you rise above your everyday state of mind, elevating you to a special place of peace and perspective.

Ritual elements need not always be exotic or difficult, by the way. In fact, I have succeeded in building a ritual routine into my life that is as natural as turning on my computer in the morning. I have built my morning interaction with my computer into a transformative experience, setting the tone for the day. Here is what I've learned about how to create a Virtual Resilience Ritual that you may find beneficial:

Virtual Resilience Ritual, Part I

Think about which computer you will use, and where. The important thing is to make an effort to find a time of day/place where you can be alone, with as few distractions as possible. The best time for you may be early in the day, before you've read an e-mail, checked Facebook, or caught the morning news.

Assuming your computer plays music, think about a CD that you find inspirational and have it loaded up and ready to go.

The final step of preparation is to make sure you have a screensaver that is meaningful to you. For instance, it may be people you love, a favorite place, a mandala . . . whatever.

That's it. You're ready to roll.

Unfocus your eyes (look at the screensaver softly) while breathing in time to the music . . . slow, deep breaths. Do this for at least five minutes. As you breathe in, take in love, faith, and whatever positive qualities the screensaver and music bring forth for you. As you breathe out, let go of worries, anxiety, or any negative emotions you'd rather not take into the day with you.

Virtual Resilience Ritual, Part II

This may well be enough for you. Many mornings, you will find yourself with your resilience replenished and spirit intact. But if you still find yourself worrying about the day, confused about a decision you need to make, or generally anxious or reactive, here is the Virtual Resilience Ritual, Part II:

Once you have competed Part I of the Ritual, set aside at least an additional half hour of uninterrupted time. Type the following questions into your computer one at a time. Answer the first question, capturing your thoughts as quickly as they come. Simply take the first thought that comes to your mind and let the words tumble onto the screen. When you've written nonstop for about two minutes, go to question two and repeat the process, and so on.

The Nine Questions of the Virtual Resilience Ritual

1. What issue is on your mind right now?
2. What outcome would you most like to achieve?
3. How have you tried to resolve this situation so far?
4. What was it about this approach that did not work?
5. What can you change about this situation?
6. What must you accept about this situation?
7. What is your greatest fear about this situation?
8. What is the truth about this situation?
9. What one thing are you now willing to do to address this issue?

Remember, the one thing you can do is not necessarily going to be an action related to mastering external circumstances. Often, in these VUCA times, it is progress enough to make the decision to wait patiently, ask for God's help, accept the ambiguity, or embrace uncertainty.

Ritual Conclusion

The ritual concludes with you sending yourself an inspirational message. Take the opportunity to summarize what you hope to take away and into your day.

May the Virtual Resilience Ritual bring you the peace and meaning that you seek.

44

Act III: Becoming Whole

by Jane Fonda

Jane Fonda is an Oscar- and Emmy-winning actress and highly successful producer. She revolutionized the fitness industry with the Jane Fonda Workout in 1982 and has sold more than 17 million copies of her fitness-focused books, videos, and recordings. She is involved with several causes and is the founder of both the Georgia Campaign for Adolescent Pregnancy Prevention and the Jane Fonda Center at Emory University. She is the author of the #1 *New York Times* best seller *My Life So Far,* and she received a Tony nomination in 2009 for her role in 33 *Variations.* She lives in Los Angeles.

The greatest potential for growth and self-realization exists in the second half of life. — Carl Jung

"How old do you feel?" someone asked me recently. I thought for a moment before answering. I wanted to really consider the question and not give a glib "I feel 40" sort of answer. "I feel 70," I said, remembering a retort of Pablo Picasso's: "It takes a long time to become young."

Ageism

A while back, I spoke to a group of adolescent girls, and when I mentioned my age, some of them winced. They whispered to me that I should not let on how old I was, because I didn't look 70. They meant this to be a compliment, but I found it sad and a little scary. Like a lot of us when we were their age, and like our culture in general, these young women viewed age as something to hide, as if youth were the pinnacle of life. Well, maybe it is the pinnacle in terms of body tautness or sperm and egg count or thickness of cartilage and bilateral activation of the parahippocampal gyrus! But I'm not the only one who wouldn't want to go back to adolescence — not for anything! It's too hard! There's too much anxiety about trying to fit in! I also wouldn't care to repeat my 20s and 30s, for that matter. For me, those years were too fraught with trying to make my mark. And heaven forbid, let's not repeat the "in between" time of the late 40s and early 50s.

For me, the "good old days" were really the "so-so old days." I spent far too much time worrying that I wasn't good enough, smart enough, thin enough, talented enough. I can honestly say that in terms of feelings of well-being, right now is the best time of my life. All those enoughnesses I worried about just don't matter as much anymore. I have come to believe that when you're actually *inside* oldness, as opposed to anticipating it from the outside, the fear subsides. You discover that you are still yourself, probably even more so.

For me, right now, this time in my life feels like I am beginning to become who I was meant to be all along. Act III isn't at all what I expected. I never envisioned myself as a happy, learning-to-be-wise older woman.

It didn't just happen. I have worked at it. I have been fortunate in myriad ways, and I have (sometimes despite myself) done what I needed to do to make the most of what I was given.

In society's terms I may be seen as "over the hill," but I've discovered a new, different, challenging landscape on the other side — a landscape filled with new depths of love, new ways of interacting with friends and strangers, new ways of expressing myself and facing setbacks, and, by the way, more hills . . . literally.

Carl Jung pondered whether "the afternoon of human life [was] merely a pitiful appendage to life's morning" or if it had a significance of its own.[1]

I believe that Rudolph Arnheim's diagrams of the arch and the staircase (which I wrote about in the Preface [of *Prime Time*]) answer Jung's question perfectly. Yes, Act III has its own significance! This is when we are meant to go deeper, to become whole. It is the time to move from ego to soul, as the spiritual teacher Ram Dass says.

[1] Carl Jung, *Modern Man in Search of a Soul*.

45

Question Everything

by Leo Sewell

Leo Sewell is an internationally recognized found-objects artist living in Philadelphia, Pennsylvania. His humorous, life-size sculptures of people and animal statues are collected by museums, corporations, and private collectors, such as Sylvester Stallone. Ripley's owns 50 of his pieces, which are displayed in Ripley's Believe It Or Not! museums around the globe.

Now that I've turned 60, I realize that rebellion, independence, contrariness, and general opposition to authority are difficult to perpetuate in middle age. Yes, I consider 60 to be only middle age, although, even with the help of preservatives and vitamin supplements, I probably will not live to be 120.

As a child of the '60s and an admitted hippie, rebellion suited me well. I peed on the Pentagon, got gassed at the Justice Department, and experimented with my fair share of sex and drugs. God, Woodstock was a blast!

Many of my generation have, to varying degrees, consciously resisted being fit into a mold. We have chosen our clothes, hair, family, friends, and other modes of taste to express who we are, deep down inside. Yet, through the decades of life, degrees of conformity are meted out by many small, but continuous decisions. Many "squares" get ground down to fit into round holes.

A good question, it seems, is: "Why?"

As I look back and around, it seems to me that employers and family are the two great forces that mold conformity. It's the lucky few on the planet who manage to retain their individuality and build successful careers expanding on their youthful rebellion. Jerry Garcia, Fidel Castro, Mick Jagger, and Allen Ginsberg are just a handful of these mavericks who come to mind.

I'm happy that I've managed to retain most of my hard edges, though far shy of the excesses of Jerry Garcia. For one thing, I haven't had a 9 to 5 job since 1970, which is probably why I look forward to continuing my art "work" for at least the next 20 years.

Choosing to become an artist fit well with the '60s scene. It is, almost by definition, the ultimate "do your own thing." I took my rebellion further, in that I attended no art classes. My selection of found objects as my medium further placed me outside the mainstream.

I've enjoyed playing with other people's "junk" as far back as I can remember. It was 50 years ago that I discovered the Navy dump near my childhood home in Annapolis, Maryland. It seems like it was just yesterday. I can still clearly visualize the dump, overflowing with mechanical parts from planes and boats. I found great joy in taking the military's castaways apart and saving each piece. As my room became more cluttered, and the puritan ethos of our home more pronounced, it occurred to me to build or combine these pieces into something new. It wasn't really about art, at this point, but play — and the joy of the objects, and creation.

This passion basically went on until college, during which I was introduced to "serious" art. My rebellion was at its peak then, and I asked, "Why not continue to play and create with these found objects and call it art?"

Marcel Duchamp (in my opinion, the greatest iconoclast and most important artist of the 20th century) became my hero and mentor. (I've heard it said that Andy Warhol explored one room in the mansion that Duchamp built. You'll get no argument from me.)

I took the time to get a graduate degree in art history, but in 1969, it was time to make my way in the world. I remember thinking that I could try to maximize my income or attempt to minimize my needs. I embraced the latter, bought a $5,000 house, and did handyman jobs to have the time to refine my art. Still, it took decades of dedication to vision and technique to reach the level of success I enjoy around the globe today as a found-objects artist.

Perhaps it is that success, however, that has entwined me with the establishment I once eschewed. Rebellion or not, I have an insurance bill that must be paid on time, a vacation home, investments, and a wife and kid. My wife has been very accepting of my nonconformity, but my 19-year-old daughter is conformity itself. How did that happen?! I love my kid to death, but I think she should spend some time listening to George Carlin.

I don't profess to know all of life's answers. For a

response to the big, mind-blowing question, "Why are we here?" I'll defer to Carlin. I will put this out there: I kinda think we're like ants on a rock. Some days, we're lucky we're not zapped by the sun through some brat's magnifying glass. Science, as explained by Karl Popper, is my god.

Since being contrary in "old" age is expected, maybe the rebellious thing for me to do is to be acceptant and nice. Let me sit with that a moment.

Moment over. Nah, not my style. At this point, though my rebellious streak has mellowed, I still want to be me. Besides, it has been scientifically proven that ornery people live longer. I have a lot of years of living yet to do. My parting words of wisdom? Be a pain in the ass and do your own thing. Life is too damn short to be pushing paper if your soul aches to go skydiving. As for me, I'll be in my studio playing with my junk.

46

Saving the Best for Last!

by Liz Pryor

Liz Pryor is quickly becoming a 21st-century voice for the modern-day American woman. After writing the book *What Did I Do Wrong? When Women Don't Tell Each Other the Friendship Is Over*, she launched her Web site, LizPryor.com, which soon became a popular online lounge for navigating the hectic daily life of American women. She delivers her practical, grounded advice in a fresh, shoot-from-the-hip style, which resonates for women from all walks of life. After recently landing the job with *Good Morning America* as their life advice guru, Pryor now writes a weekly column for ABC *News*, dispenses advice in letter form, and appears on air. She speaks at national women's conventions and has more books in the works. The single mother of three teenagers, Pryor lives in Los Angeles, California, and happily commutes to New York City for her new job.

Life as we collectively know it has changed exponentially in the last decade. Advancement, information overload, and an amped-up pace have forever shifted the foundation of how we live in the world. As a result, for most of us the appeal of the term "retirement" is rising by the day. However, a few snags are often felt by those about to close the door on a lifetime of work. Many of us face a major struggle that stems from our having spent years adamantly dedicated to being creatures of habit and pattern.

We search long and hard to find ways to nurture and maintain our lives as we build them over the years. We put on our blinders and go at our lives full speed in whatever way works for us. It's what a lot of us know how to do. And in our effort to keep the momentum and not feel as though we're sinking, we create a sort of steel-wall mentality about how we go about life. We all do it to a degree, making our way in our own little countries that we call our lives. This way of functioning helps us to cope and protects us from feeling that things will fall apart. On one hand, it works in our favor and becomes the shield by which we live; on the other hand, it can become an obstacle that stops us from being able to ever recreate our view of life. And that's when our habitual way of seeing things can become debilitating.

In order to fully live the kind of life we deserve, the steel walls that narrow our thinking need to come down. Walking into retirement, we have an opportunity to reset our lives, and that begins with resetting ourselves.

In theory, we've been trading in the hours of our days for the money we need to live. Whatever our individual experiences have been — whether we've spent 50 years at the same place, moved ourselves all over the world, worked from home, made millions, or just gotten by — the one common denominator and inescapable reality for all of us at this time in life is what will be demanded from us when we get to the new door. The demand requires the kind of work from which most of us would run as fast as we can, if we could — because it involves looking inside ourselves, at who we've become, who we once were, and who we want to be as we move forward. It's the inevitable self-search for the truth. The "in one ear, out the other" kind of statement that in this case requires a listener. In order to move to where we want to go, we have to know what we're dealing with, and what it is that keeps us from being who we are and who we want to be.

How much have we buried, lost, discarded, gained, learned, or gathered over time? And when was the last time we really checked in with ourselves, going within to our deepest core? Can we stand who we've become enough to be with ourselves without the kind of distractions to which we have become so accustomed? It's a bummer, but the truth is we can't delegate or outsource our own self-search; we actually have to go at it ourselves in a way most of us may never have. Reaching in to look at the accuracy and truth of who we are is crucial at this stage in the game, in order for the next road to be what we want it to be. It's a chance to take the walls down and to see who we've become. Whatever information we gather, it's important we know it.

And after the arduous task of assessing ourselves, and then coming out with some truths and revelations about our lives, we are obligated to check in with the king honcho boss of all bosses — the ultimate worst and best critic we have — ourselves. Regardless of what comes of our search, completing an order this tall is imperative to good living. Instead of being the person who says, "If I could I would," you can come closer to being the person who states, "I do and I can."

Learn yourself as well as you possibly can. And

remember, the modifications that come with retiring will surface pretty immediately, and are amazingly appealing.

Your alarm clock will no longer have a purpose and your neighbor may now have a name you remember. The moments you share with the people you love will linger in your thoughts. You will finish a book; you will no longer have reason to procrastinate. You'll learn what was true and untrue about the things you thought you would do if you had the time. You'll walk your dog for insanely long periods of time. You will pay less for a movie you now have time to see. Your ability to be patient will return (except in traffic). You will experience moments you never noticed before. This is the beginning of a view you haven't seen in a long time — take a slow look and enjoy it.

47

Ask the Big Questions

by Tina B. Tessina, Ph.D.

Tina B. Tessina, Ph.D., is a licensed psychotherapist in South California, with over 30 years' experience in counseling individuals and couples. She is the author of 13 books in 17 languages, including *It Ends With You: Grow Up and Out of Dysfunction* and her newest, *Lovestyles: How to Celebrate Your Differences.* She publishes the "Happiness Tips from Tina" e-mail newsletter, and the "Dr. Romance Blog." Online, she is "Dr. Romance" with columns at Divorce360.com, Wellsphere.com, and Shine from Yahoo!, and she appears on radio and TV. She tweets @tinatessina and is on Facebook at www.facebook.com/tinatessina and www.facebook.com/#!/DrRomanceBlog.

P erhaps the most important lesson I've learned is that a meaningful life is about growing your soul — and it happens slowly, in the process of engaging life.

My own soul was battered early when my whole family died during my teenage years, and I was left alone, terrified, without money, education, or an idea of what to do. I just stumbled through the days, months, and years, too afraid to feel what I feared was inside me, grasping at the wrong lifelines and clinging to the wrong people until, divorced, bereft, suicidal, and single, at age 27, I entered therapy and began to develop my soul through exploring my feelings. This decision saved my life and became the basis for a personal renaissance. As I searched for meaning and purpose, I began to understand I'd been put on Earth to learn and grow, and to use what I'd learned in the process of healing myself to help others. Now that I've just turned 62, I find that sense of purpose is still serving me well and has been the source of many blessings.

As a child with no religious training, but growing up in the beautiful surroundings of the Catskill Mountains, I sensed a Power behind the workings of the Universe, which has inspired me to yearn and aspire, comforted me in times of pain, and provided clarity and direction when I needed it. Human relationships bruise, batter, and comfort me, and teach resilience and humility. Love urges my soul to blossom and grow; compassion causes it to blur at the edges. And so I learn to accept others as they are.

Every day, I have the delight and privilege of loving Richard, my husband, a real, human, fallible man. My friends are an equal blessing and challenge. We can be cranky, we occasionally hurt each other's feelings, and we don't always say the right thing. But we are here for each other when we're really needed, we do our best to be caring and kind, and we forgive each other's imperfections.

Most of my clients come to me, not searching for the meaning of life, but focused on some crisis in their lives: a relationship disaster; marriage or family problems; lack of direction and motivation; some huge loss for which they're grieving; an emotional problem, such as anxiety or depression; or perhaps for help in recovering from an addiction. As we sort through the crisis, handle immediate problems, get everything settled down, and then embark on an extended process of figuring out what happened and what must change, their life gets easier.

Then, frequently, a patient asks: "Now that I'm in charge of myself and have a lot of extra energy, and life is a lot easier and my relationships are working, it feels like I'm missing something. The question is: *What am I doing here?*"

Once the basics of life are established and understood, many people need a sense of meaning and a higher sense of purpose than just survival. When self-confidence and self-esteem are in place, we need a challenge to feel satisfied, a way to express our uniqueness and individuality — to ourselves, to friends, and to the world.

If your life's purpose is not evident to you already, how do you find out what it is? Where does a sense of purpose come from? It comes from within and cannot be imposed or chosen from outside. Your purpose may be your livelihood, or it may have nothing to do with how you make a living. Your purpose may be a simple one, like making a good, healthy life for yourself and your children, or it may be more dramatic and based on what you've learned by healing your own childhood experience. Inner purpose has the power to transform anxiety, anger, fear, and rage into powerful, life-affirming action. A life's purpose gives you the means to control your destiny, no matter what the force of the hardships you have incurred.

Most of the world's spiritual thinkers agree that we all have the wisdom to guide each of us — if we just know how to listen and to trust what we learn. Purpose may make itself clear in one instant flash or gradually — by following clues, one at a time. Whether you get insight all at once or a piece at a time, work and experience are required to nurture it. Inner wisdom is not rational or practical in nature, but intuitive and spiritual. It can provide a way to see the big picture or a more detached and objective viewpoint of the issues and problems of life. Each new idea must be tested through practical use to see how it works. Step by step, using both intuitive wisdom and clear thinking, you can bring your inner motivation to the surface and use it to create what you want. Inspiration expressed through action will develop the meaning of your own life.

Here's how I expressed my own life experience, in a poem called "Grace":

Life
is worked
On a wheel
Sloppy, slippery
Formless base clay
Rising coaxed, caressed,
Coerced and beaten into shape

Tested in passion's consuming fire
Until worthy to catch and hold
A bit of the liquid grace
Pouring unceasingly over us.

48

Be Happy While You Are Alive Because You Are a Long Time Dead!

by Ernie J. Zelinski

Ernie J. Zelinski is an international best-selling author, professional speaker, and prosperity life coach specializing in creating inspirational life-changing books, Web sites, e-books, and seminars. He is the author of the international best sellers *The Joy of Not Working* (over 250,000 copies sold) and *How to Retire Happy, Wild, and Free* (over 150,000 copies sold), two life-changing books that have helped hundreds of thousands of individuals around the world achieve a more wholesome life. Zelinski's core message — that ordinary people can attain extraordinary results and make a big difference in this world — is at the heart of his work. He deeply believes in the powers of creativity and well-intentioned action as the most important elements for attaining personal prosperity and financial freedom. Meet him at www.erniezelinski.com, www.retirement-cafe.com, and www.how-to-retire-happy.com.

Think about this quietly and carefully: Years from now, as you review your life, what will you regret not having done? Clearly, it won't be to have worked longer and harder at your career. Just as telling, it won't be that you didn't watch more TV.

No doubt you don't want to leave this world with songs unsung that you would like to have sung. Thus, shouldn't you start singing those songs today? Most people go to their graves regretting things they haven't done. The easiest way to become one of them is by joining society's chorus instead of singing your own songs.

Some things are important and some aren't. It's essential that you know how to tell the difference. If your life is a good case study in perpetual stress and turmoil, there's no point in declaring: "I may not be here for a good time, but I'm here for a long time!" What's the point of being here for a long time if you aren't going to enjoy yourself?

Henry David Thoreau warned us: "Oh, God, to reach the point of death and realize you have never lived at all." Instead of wasting your time regretting the things you didn't do in your life, use the time to pursue some of them now. Most people who reach 65 or beyond look back on their lives in later years with regret. They wish they had set their priorities differently. They wish they hadn't been as concerned about the little things and had spent more time doing the things they had wanted to do.

In a recent survey, a number of individuals, all over 60 years old, were asked what advice they would give themselves if they had life to live over. It may do you good to pay attention to the following six of their suggestions: (1) Take the time to find what you really want to do with your life. (2) Take more risks. (3) Lighten up and don't take life so seriously. (4) It's best to suffer from the Peter Pan syndrome — relive your younger days. What were your dreams when you were young? (5) Be more patient. (6) Live the moment more.

The good news is that it is never too late in your life — or too early, for that matter — to change direction, to be what you might have been. Of course, those who are resistant to change at 30 will be even more resistant to change at 93. Don't be one of them. If you keep doing what you have been doing, you will keep getting what you have always been getting — well into infinity and beyond.

Some people die at 45, but they have experienced a heck of a lot more happiness in those 45 years than others who have lived to be 90 or 100. The reason is that they mastered the moment while they were alive. In this regard, a Scottish proverb advises, "Be happy while you are alive because you are a long time dead." For independent-minded individuals, freedom contributes to a lot of their happiness. But freedom isn't the ability to do what others are doing. On the contrary, freedom is the ability to do what the majority in society are afraid of doing on their own. Only when you are able to be creative and significantly different — even wildly eccentric — will you be free.

You don't want to end up on your deathbed pleading, "Lord, give me one more shot and I'll give it all I got." As the saying goes, "Get a life." Not just an ordinary life. Get a great life. Get a focused, satisfying, balanced life instead of one filled with nothing but watching TV and other passive activities.

Spare lots of time for family, friends, and leisure. Most important — don't forget to spare time for yourself. Nothing that is human should be foreign to you. Make the small pleasures in life your biggest priorities. Wise people realize that the simple pleasures — nature, health, music, friendship, etc. — are the most satisfying.

Have some perpetual small enjoyment in which you indulge daily. Never miss it, regardless of how busy you are. This will do wonders for your mental well-being. Indeed, it will do more for your happiness than acquiring the biggest and best of possessions.

Call forth the best you can muster for living life to the fullest, regardless of how limited your funds. The Greeks say, "When you are poor, it is important to have a good time." So take the opportunity to drink quality wine or champagne with your friends at least once a week. This is especially important when you have something to celebrate — and even much more important when you don't!

Freedom and happiness are easier to attain than you think. Take your lesson from children. Don't fret about the future. Don't regret the past. Live only in the present. The happiness you have at any moment is the only happiness you can ever experience. Reminisce about your great yesterdays, hope for many interesting tomorrows, but, above all, ensure that you live today. Consider each day you haven't laughed, played, and celebrated your life to be wasted. "Keep a green tree in your heart and perhaps the songbird will come," states a Chinese proverb. You were given three special gifts when you were born: the gifts of life, love, and laughter. Learn to share these gifts with the rest of the world — and the rest of the world will play happily with you.

In the same vein, don't lose touch with the craziness within yourself. Often one gets a reputation for mental stability simply because one doesn't have enough courage to make a fool of oneself. Is it more important to live with zest or to have people think nice things about you? The point is, if you want to be truly alive, forget about what people think.

Always question what your neighbors say or do or think. It is unwise to use the conduct of the majority in society as a viable precedent for your own life. Do so and you will be setting yourself up for much disappointment and disillusionment. What the majority pursue are seldom the things that bring happiness, satisfaction, and freedom to any individual's life.

Resist accepting society's way of living as the right one. Your primary duty is to be yourself. Invent a lifestyle that expresses who you are. In the end, there is no right way of living. There is only your way.

Determine your direction clearly before you choose the speed at which you want to travel. In Western society, most people today are in a hurry to get to places not worth going. Speed in life doesn't count as much as direction. Indeed, where there is no direction, speed doesn't count at all.

To a large degree, freedom entails nonattachment to what others can't do without. Zen masters tell us that people become imprisoned by what they are most attached to: Cars. Houses. Money. Egos. Identities. Let go of your attachment to these things and you will be set free.

Give up the idea of finding the seven secrets to living happily ever after. The secrets for living a full, rewarding, fulfilled, and enlightened life are not really secrets. These principles have been passed down through the ages, but the majority of humans tend to discount them and follow principles that don't work. "In the end these things matter most," revealed Buddha. "How well did you love? How fully did you live? How deeply did you learn to let go?"

When a friend offers to spend time with you either today or tomorrow, always choose today. No individual gets out of this world alive, so the ideal time to love, and laugh with your friends is always today. Spending as much time as possible with your friends is solid proof of your intention to live your life now — while you have it — and be dead later — when you are!

It's essential that you identify the resources most important for your present-day happiness. When money is lost, a little is lost. When time is lost, much more is lost. When health is lost, practically everything is gone. And when creative spirit is lost, there is nothing left.

Get the picture? Life is a game in many ways. It is important to play the game here and now, in the present. Find a version of the game worth playing — a version that you truly enjoy. Ensure that you laugh and have fun, even when the score is not in your favor. You have to play the game of life with gusto, and if you get really good at it, you will miraculously transform your world — forever! After all, it's all in how you play the game, isn't it?

Section

6

FAMILY MATTERS

49

Honey, We Need to Talk!

by Dorian Mintzer, M.S.W., Ph.D.

Dorian Mintzer, M.S.W., Ph.D., is an LICSW and a licensed psychologist, life planning coach, retirement transition coach, couples relationship coach, executive coach, writer, teacher, and speaker. She is a licensed third age coach and a 2Young2Retire certified facilitator. She is founder of the Boomers and Beyond Special Interest Group for Interdisciplinary Professionals. She utilizes her life experiences and expertise in adult development and life planning in her work with helping individuals and couples develop their "voice" and clarify their goals, values, and priorities as they navigate the second half of life. She is coauthor, with Roberta Taylor, of *The Couples Retirement Puzzle: 10 Must-Have Conversations for Transitioning to the Second Half of Life*. Her web sites are www.revolutionizeretirement.com and www.couplesretirementpuzzle.com.

In the 21st century we're living longer and the concept of retirement is changing. The old notion of "retirement" has focused on "retiring from" and often has connoted decline and "going downhill." We're now living longer and, hopefully, with better health.

Many people don't want to stop working and others can't stop working so they don't outlive their money. With people living longer, it's important for couples to talk about how they want to live the potentially 25-plus additional years. These retirement transition years provide an opportunity for new possibilities: for self-reflection and discovery as you decide "what's next?"— perhaps thinking about some interests you had put on the "back burner" while you were attending to building your own career and/or focusing on the growth and development of others in your life. You may now be thinking about what's on your own "vision list" of things you want to do and experience. There may be a normal questioning of "Is this all there is?" or "What am I missing?" There may also be worries about "Who am I without my work?"

It's hard enough to think about "what's next?" for yourself — but it can get more complicated if you're part of a couple. You may not be on the same page as your partner about your dreams, priorities, goals, and timetables regarding such issues as where you'll live now that you're retired — or what kind of lifestyle you want to have. You might also have differences about:

- your finances

- your changing roles and identity

- your responsibility and obligations to your children, grandchildren, or other relatives

- your relationship with friends

- your health, wellness, and energy levels

- how much time you want to spend together or apart

- intimacy and sexuality

What gives you purpose and meaning may be different from what satisfies your partner. "Yikes, what can I do about this?" you might ask. The answer is: *Talk with your partner.* These may be difficult conversations — but they, and many others, are important conversations to have — the earlier the better. If you haven't been talking about these issues, it's time to start now! Being able to find ways to talk with each other about this next stage of life can take a lot of stress out of the relationship and help you approach the future with some planning and goals rather than just allowing things to happen by default. So much in life is out of our control that it's important to control the parts we can.

It sounds simple enough — but actually it's not so

simple for many couples. Many couples avoid these conversations for a variety of reasons. What gets in the way? One of the perennial problems is not being able to find the time to discuss these serious topics in the midst of busy lives. Other obstacles may be fear of bringing up issues when you assume you'll disagree and you want to avoid conflict, or not wanting to think ahead since it feels too scary to think about the end of life, or not knowing how to bring up difficult issues. It doesn't necessarily mean you have a "bad relationship," but that you've developed some ways to avoid important conversations and don't know how to turn that around.

It's not unusual for some people to get caught in their positions about issues; they dig in their heels and refuse to budge, creating a win-lose dynamic in the relationship. This often results in resentment and anger for the person who feels that his or her opinions "don't count." Does this sound or feel familiar? If so, you're not alone. The key is to develop ways to talk together so that you find opportunities for compromise and ultimately find what are called win-win solutions where both of your needs are taken into account.

A book I coauthored with Roberta Taylor, *The Couples Retirement Puzzle: 10 Must-Have Conversations for Transitioning to the Second Half of Life*, provides a "roadmap" to help couples learn how to have these important conversations. Some tips for effective communication include sharing your own thoughts and feelings by using what are called "I" statements and avoiding "you" statements, which often feel blaming and attacking. Set a safe place to talk — with a time limit and without distractions such as the telephone, TV, or computer.

Most important, learn to listen and appreciate what you hear from your partner, agree to disagree, and don't make assumptions. It's easy to think that you know what your partner is going to say, so you "tune out" after the first few words. It's helpful to check out what you've heard before you respond. A particularly meaningful question to ask might be, "Tell me why this is so important to you?" You may not agree — but it's helpful to understand why the issue matters so much to your partner. The goal is to open up a space for the "we" of the relationship, where you can move from your entrenched positions to the possibility of compromise. It won't be a ledger that balances out each time, but it's beneficial if it incorporates some of each of your wishes. For example, now that you're retired, you might want to spend winters in Florida and your partner may want to be near the grandchildren in New York. You might say, "Let's try out living separately and then visiting together once a month during the winter and see how that works." Good communication can lead to some creative possibilities for this next stage of life. The goal is to find the essence of the "we" of your relationship while still honoring each of you as individuals. A challenge? Yes! Possible? Definitely!

50

The Spouse in Retirement

by Dave D'Antoni

Since retiring at 60 from his career as an engineer and corporate executive, Dave D'Antoni has lived in Naples, Florida, with his wife, Sue Ann, and their miniature dachshund, Rudy. They have two grown children. His book *The Globe-Trotting Golfer's Guide to Retirement* is packed with practical wisdom on planning for, and enjoying, retirement.

My wife doesn't mind if I hang around the house.
She only gets mad if I try to come inside.
— a retiree who wishes to remain anonymous

While retiring from work and entering an unstructured world is a big step for you, if you're a guy, the fact that you will now be entering your wife's domain can be an even bigger adjustment for her. As the result of your retirement, she now gets a lot more of you and a fixed, and likely reduced, income to boot. What a deal!

For a woman who's worked outside the home all or most of her married life, this doesn't seem to be as much of an issue. She probably knows what she wants to do on Day One of her retirement. She's got her activities planned, for the day, for the week, maybe even for the year . . . because, even though she's been working full-time, she's also likely to have been in charge of making the family's plans all along. If the two of you retire at the same time, she's probably going to act in much the same way as she always has. But what if she's not ready to retire and you are? She loves her job and has just (finally) made vice-president or partner and likes the office with the window. Or what if you want to move to Costa Rica for the balmy weather and the deep-sea fishing and she wants to stay in Cleveland, where she's spent decades building a network of friends and there's great shopping and a world-class philharmonic orchestra?

Retirement issues are a huge but not generally acknowledged source of marital discord. To avoid this, discuss frankly and frequently how both of you feel about the adjustments brought about by your retirement — and don't stop at the financial issues. They're the easy part.

A husband's retirement will be much more traumatic for a woman if it involves a permanent or even a seasonal move to a new location. In this case, she has to give up her friends and routine and start her life over with only you. Talk about tough!

My wife struggled mightily with these upcoming changes in her life as I got closer and closer to retirement. One day, when I got home from work, she said, "I figured it out. I just need to get into the bucket."

It seems that on that day, there was an interview with Ellen DeGeneres in our local newspaper. Ellen told a story about her move into a new house. Her old house had an inground fish pond. She enjoyed watching the fish in the pond so much that she had a similar pond built at her new house.

When it came time for her to move, she tried to catch the fish in a bucket to relocate them to their new home. This proved to be very difficult. The fish had no way of knowing that the new pond was bigger and better than their current pond. They only knew that they were secure and happy where they were.

Ellen pointed out that people are often like her fish.

We are comfortable with where we are and what we do. We are not willing to try different things or to take chances, because change is scary. But sometimes you just need to "get into the bucket" and move on.

By the way, my wife did "get into the bucket" and is very glad she did.

Retirement is not an easy change for couples, because both husband and wife need to get comfortable with their new lives. Even if you don't move, each of you will experience a substantial change of routine, including restructuring every hour of your day. Each of you needs to make new friends, both together and separately, and new rules need to be developed.

As a gag gift, I tried to capture a common spousal sentiment in words and had them inscribed on refrigerator magnets that I gave to the wives of retiring friends. The magnets read:

I am not your secretary,

I am not your mother,

You will have to do it yourself.

Several recipients of these magnets said that after a while, when their husbands asked them to do something, they only had to point to the refrigerator (and to watch the way the poor guys, heads dropped). Predictably, my retiring friends were not all that thrilled with my gift.

In our case, the new rules were never formalized or actually even discussed. Nonetheless, we both came to understand them. Below are the ones that I now follow after having been critiqued and criticized over the past seven years:

1. The newspapers are hers first. I can look at them only after she is finished.

2. Breakfast is served at home only if I make it for myself or if I wait until she gets up and is ready to eat.

3. Lunch at home is out of the question.

4. My study door is to be kept shut when I am using the speaker phone or watching CNBC or sports or a movie, etc.

5. If I ever attempt to help organize my wife's activities or her parts of the house (which include everything but my study and the garage), I am reminded that if I need to boss people around I should get a job.

My relationship with my wife has gone very well in retirement since I learned these unwritten rules. She is busy with her friends playing golf and mah-jongg and shopping. I am enjoying my friends at my "adult day care center," also known as the golf club.

As a couple we love to go to the movies with friends or by ourselves, and we also eat out with friends or alone. Occasionally we even play golf together. And we enjoy travel. We take two major trips a year, and we've already been on ocean and river cruises, international land tours, and an African safari.

You can only have a happy and successful retirement *if* your wife is also happy with her new situation. Do not minimize the importance of her happiness. Work hard to stay out of her space and help her through this big change in her life.

51

Do What You Love

by Aleta St. James

Aleta St. James, author of *Life Shift: Let Go and Live Your Dream*, believes that impossible dreams are possible if you are willing to become the person your dream calls you to be. She also believes that beauty is power, so look as good on the outside as you feel on the inside, and know that menopause means "winding up, instead of winding down, baby." St. James became a true example of these beliefs when she delivered healthy twins at the age of 57.

At age 54, my grandmother, Nicoletta Bianchino, gave birth to my mother, the last of 13 children in an Italian-American family. My mother was the only child born in America and the jewel in my grandmother's eyes. I grew up thinking this was normal. Never once did I think it odd or far-fetched when, at the age of 49, I began to think seriously of starting my own family. My grandmother had children at a later age. Why was it strange to think that I could give birth to healthy twins at 57 and have the energy to take care of them?

Nicoletta, with her wise wisdom, inspired me with heartfelt stories of her courage and determination. She dramatically told me about her beloved father, who was one of the wealthiest men in Badi, Italy. She was brought up with servants and tutors, and she was courted by many eligible suitors. Nicoletta's young heart was captured, though, when she heard my grandfather, Fidel Bianchino, serenading her with his soulful voice. One moonlit night, throwing caution to the wind, she eloped with the handsome Fidel. Her heartbroken father screamed for vengeance and called in the militia, condemning Fidel to almost certain death.

Nicoletta, who might have spent the rest of her days in a palace, hid in fear with my grandfather in a wine barrel — until she appeared three months later on her father's doorstep, armed with a marriage certificate and visibly pregnant. My grandmother, in true Puccini fashion, pleaded for her husband's life. My great-grandfather's cold heart melted. "*Figlia mia* (my darling daughter)," he said, "so be it." And he called off the troops.

My grandmother moved into one of the poorest houses in town, where she lived just above the chickens, with their only cow. She never looked back, and raised 12 of her 13 children there, giving birth to the last after she moved to America in 1922. I think that having this child in her 50s gave her an added zest for life that seemed to grow through her 60s, 70s, and on, along with the joy she got from each of her 20 grandchildren.

As I enter my 60s, I find myself smiling and thinking of my grandmother, while changing diapers and singing "Elmo" songs. It's true that once you have children, life is never the same. These two little munchkins have totally detonated my fixed routine and forced me out of my comfort zone. I have now mastered the three-minute shower and the bimonthly manicure. My new mantra is: "Go with the Flow."

My children have opened up my heart to experience a greater, more unselfish depth of love, and they have brought out fierce feelings of protectiveness — as they go through their colds, high temperatures, and bumps on their heads. What am I going to do when they are teenagers, and Francesca comes home with purple hair and Gian wants to ride a motorcycle? Sometimes I wonder how I am ever going to survive this. And then, when I think of the crazy things I did in the '60s,

I wonder how my mother ever survived me! It has brought a whole different meaning to Mother's Day.

As an emotional healer and success coach over the past 25 years, I have helped thousands of people realize their deepest dreams and desires. I believe that it is never too late to live your dreams. What keeps us stuck as we get older is the fear that we don't deserve to receive what we want. We think that we are too old, too tired, or not beautiful enough to have the supportive relationship, the financial freedom, and the meaningful, joyful life we desire.

I am convinced that — just as it was in my grandmother's time — it's the enthusiasm we have for life that keeps us going. That enthusiasm comes only from following our hearts. So many of us get so bogged down in negative feelings and thoughts about ourselves, which are steeped in the disappointments of the past, that we stop dreaming and doing the things that really make us happy.

Having children later in life may not be what you had in mind for your 60s, but the message is still the same. Like my grandmother Nicoletta, you must find something you love to do, and you must be passionate about it. It will fuel you with the joy and enthusiasm that will keep you winding up, not down. You are never too old to live your dreams — if you're willing to get out of your comfort zone, go with the flow, and feel like you deserve to receive what you desire.

Your desires are important; they lead you to your destiny. I'd like to leave you with this thought from my book, *Life Shift*: "No dream is too big; you just need to become the person it challenges you to be."

52

Go Fishing with Your Grandchildren

by Robert E. Rich, Jr.

Robert E. Rich, Jr., president of Rich Products Corp., in Buffalo, New York, is the author of Fish Fights and The Fishing Club: Brothers and Sisters of the Angle. One of three members of the South Florida Fishing Hall, he splits his fishing time between Buffalo and the Florida Keys.

Bill Dance surprised me the other day. We were chatting about our fishing lives and our families, and Dance, the Great One, the world's most recognized bass fisherman, said to me, "You know, the biggest thrill I've had in fishing is being there when all of my children, and my first grandchild, caught their first fish."

Now here's an angler who's fished and won nearly every bass tournament there is. But what he remembers most about the sport is the excitement of his grandchild's first catch.

I guess I shouldn't have been so surprised. I had just finished the manuscript of my newest book. *The Fishing Club: Brothers and Sisters of the Angle* explores the reasons why different anglers fish. During the process, I discovered that almost all of my subjects learned the sport from their grandparents — not their parents, but their grandparents!

Given the economic and time pressures on most families today, and the prevalence of two wage-earner parents per family, it makes sense that grandparents would introduce the kids to the joys of fishing.

After all, it is the grandparents who generally have more time on their hands, as well as more patience to deal with the young ones — at least over short periods of time! Dance shared with me that his grandfather, a doctor who lived in Lynchburg, Tennessee, taught him how to fish. He said he'll never forget their trips together on the river.

John Bailey, one of the most talented and prolific fishing authors in the world, also learned from a grandparent. Bailey loves to reflect on the beginning of his fishing career, when he was growing up in England. In his case, it was his grandmother who took him to a lake and fastened a bobber to his line. After a while, the bobber went down, thrilling him! He'd snared his first fish! With his grandmother cheering him on, Bailey reeled in his line — revealing a fish cleverly disguised as a large green turtle. Bailey has fond memories of this experience. It helped him to know his grandmother better, he said.

One of my pals, Scott Keller, a trout guide out West, smiles when he talks about how his grandfather taught him to fish in California. The two went out on a small lake in a little boat. After they anchored up, Keller's grandfather took out a pound of cheese and showed his young grandson how to roll small cheese balls that they then tossed into the water.

After about five minutes, which probably seemed like an eternity to Keller at this young age, his grandfather hooked a cheese ball to his line. Not surprisingly, Keller caught his first fish. "He showed me right then how to 'match the hatch,'" Keller told me, smiling. "I decided that day that not only did I love to fish, but that I wanted to be a fishing guide."

Even President George H. W. Bush remembers learning how to fish from his grandfather, off the coast of Maine. "His boat was called *Tomboy*," he recalls, "and sometimes when I got older, he'd let me drive. I guess that's where I got my love of the ocean and fishing and boats." Are you surprised that this very busy man, during his tenure as probably the most powerful man on Earth, still made time to fish? I'm not.

Lastly, there's William Bradley, one of the most interesting people I've met while fishing. An older gentleman, Bradley fishes every day in the summer from his favorite pier in my hometown, Buffalo, New York. Mr. Bradley's ancestors were slaves in South Carolina, where he grew up. A twinkle came to his eye when he talked about his grandfather waking him up early to go fishing.

"Is that because that's when the fish bit the best?" I asked him.

"Not actually," he replied. "He just liked to get up and sneak out early, so he didn't have to work in those cotton fields."

And then Bradley said something that echoed a feeling that I have. "My grandfather was a wonderful man," he said, "and I'll never forget him. I want to teach my grandchildren to fish just like he taught me."

There is a great deal of precedent in literature for the old to teach the young to fish. In his novel *The Old Man and the Sea*, for example, Ernest Hemingway penned a loving relationship between the old fisherman, Santiago, and the five-year-old boy, Manolin, he took out fishing with him. My favorite lines from this novel read:

> *Everything about him was old except his eyes and they were the same color as the sea and were cheerful and undefeated . . . the old man had taught the boy to fish and the boy loved him.*

As I reflected on this one night, getting ready for bed and feeling a bit "long of tooth," I thought of my seven young grandkids, and how pleased I was that many of them would be old enough to go fishing with me this summer.

Then a cold thought entered my mind and went right to my gut. It was quickly followed by thoughts even more painful. Maybe my grandchildren won't remember the experience, or maybe it will become a blur. Maybe I'll become irrelevant. Or worse, after I'm gone, maybe they won't remember me.

Thumbing again through *The Old Man and the Sea*, I came across a conversation between the old man and the boy about their first fishing trip together:

"Can you really remember or did I just tell it to you?"

"I remember everything from when we first went together." The old man looked at him with his sun-burned, confident loving eyes.

That's it, I thought, as I got into bed and turned out the lights. Seven new anglers are going fishing with their grandpa this summer. Isn't it ironic that grandchildren, whose births at first make us feel so very old, can suddenly make us feel young again — through the student/teacher dynamic — as we quest for fish?

At the end of the day, fishing may not provide us with immortality. But it will give us a chance to pass along a pastime/sport to our grandkids and provide them with memories they'll never forget. Some of those memories will be of us.

Sixty-five things to do when you retire: One of them should be to take your grandchildren fishing.

Section

GO FOR IT!

53

Fall in Love Again

by Sharon Gilchrest O'Neill, Ed.S., LMFT

Sharon Gilchrest O'Neill, Ed.S., LMFT, is a licensed marriage and family therapist and the author of A *Short Guide to a Happy Marriage*, *Sheltering Thoughts About Loss and Grief*, and *Lur'ning: 147 Inspiring Thoughts for Learning on the Job*. She has worked for over 30 years, both in private practice and the corporate setting, helping her clients to examine assumptions, think creatively, and build upon strengths. O'Neill holds three degrees in psychology, is a clinical member of AAMFT, and maintains a private practice in Westchester, New York. She is often called on as an expert by a variety of print/online publications, including the *New York Times*, the *Boston Globe*, and the *Wall Street Journal*. www.ashortguidetoahappymarriage.com

Love is a longing. It is the desire to have that special person in our lives, the one who understands us and knows us better than anyone else. Whether you are moving into your retirement years with a 40-year marriage, or starting with a new partner, these relationship years can be tremendously fulfilling. They will likely not look and feel like what has come before. Be ready to open yourself to possibilities and to rally all your capability for change. Expect that you will be operating outside of your comfort zone. Falling in love again with your spouse or starting with a new love is ultimately a gift you give yourself. It doesn't just happen.

Research suggests that to challenge ourselves intellectually as we age can prolong that capability for change. Accordingly, we should challenge ourselves within our intimate relationships. Emotional well-being will increase and health risks will decrease. What could be better?

Don't let the past keep you down. Yes, love is complicated and you've most likely had your share of difficult times. But you also have more experience, maturity, and wisdom to draw upon, and are beyond all the early developmental stages of kids and careers that so easily get in the way. This is the perfect time for intimate beginnings and focusing on your partner.

So, just how will you focus? Here's a little guidance to get you started.

Life in retirement continues to be a journey of personal growth. Seriously consider and reflect upon earlier criticism about how you participated in relationships. You can count on there being some solid truth in what you heard. Watch out for those weak points as you pursue a new love or take the time to rediscover what first attracted you to the love of your last 40 years. But this time, steer clear of the trap of relying on assumptions. Ask questions.

Walk in your partner's shoes every day. Take time to understand your partner's perspectives. Be curious about what he or she is thinking and feeling. Become inspired by this person, who can be so vital in your life. Glance through a book that you see excites your partner, even if it doesn't quite excite you. You may learn something new or interesting, but more important, these kinds of gestures bring you closer to your partner because they are gifts of loving empathy.

Give and Take. Give and Take. This is the mantra of relationships. Do your part. Be nicer to your partner than to anyone else. And don't forget that simple, old-fashioned manners go a long way. Actually, why not set yourself the goal of being more often on the positive side of the Give and Take balance sheet. Intimate relationships are built on the daily accumulation of moments of sharing and caring.

Be honest with yourself. You do have time now to be

more patient and to explore life with your partner. Open up a bit more than you've been used to — share what you're thinking and feeling to expand your comfort zones. Discover new ways of spending time together. Try on new roles. If you've never made the meals, pull out a cookbook — maybe even take a class — and give it a try. If you've never done any of the yard work or gardening, show up one afternoon and lend your partner a hand. You may be surprised at just how meaningful a new role can become.

What is sexuality about at 65 and beyond? Whatever you and your partner want it to be. And as tough as it may still seem at this stage of life, there is only one way to make it happen, and that's with conversation and having the courage to risk sharing your thoughts about sex. If you know you haven't been too good at this, ask your partner for help in getting started and stay committed to the process. Begin by expressing some simple desires: you might like to share fantasies, receive a massage, have a quickie now and then in the morning, or sleep naked together more often.

What is true about relationships at this stage of life is that sexual satisfaction depends more on the overall quality of the relationship. So, all that you do counts toward enhanced intimacy; nothing is wasted. A quick hug, a special touch, listening during a difficult time, a thoughtful comment, or help with the dinner party. It really does all add up.

You and your partner will need to understand the expectations and assumptions you each bring to your retirement years. There will be new life options and opportunities to consider. Here are just a few: Will you downsize? Where will you live? How much will you travel? How often will you visit family and babysit for grandkids? What do you need in order to pursue your goals? Old dreams need to be updated or discarded, and new ones revealed.

Challenge yourself as a couple to think outside the "retirement box." Try on new ideas, and be creative and flexible in your thinking. Brainstorm together by growing and building on each other's ideas. Use active listening skills and suspend judgment while you are in the midst of learning about your partner's hopes and dreams.

And lastly, celebrate falling in love again with an experience that sets this time apart. Maybe a special gift for the two of you or a surprising new adventure. Always be making new memories to reminisce about in the future.

54

Olympic Dreams: It's Never Too Late

by Ruth Heidrich, Ph.D.

Ruth Heidrich, Ph.D., although retired, is an author, speaker, nutritionist, talk-show host, and triathlete. Living in Honolulu, Hawaii, she trains in running, biking, and swimming all year round. Still competing, she's won more than 900 medals and was named one of the "Ten Fittest Women in North America" by Living Fit magazine. Her books include A Race For Life, which details her struggle to beat her fast metastasizing cancer; The Race For Life Cookbook; and Senior Fitness. Her Web site is www. RuthHeidrich.com.

"And in first place overall . . ." the announcer's voice boomed over the PA system at the finish of the Senior Olympics triathlon. I heard my name and excitedly ran up to the stage to collect my gold medal. As I stood on the stage, I choked back tears, overwhelmed by just how far I had come — from having breast cancer to being the winner of a triathlon!

It was such a contrast from another day when I heard my name called, only that time it was in a doctor's office to receive the results of a biopsy of a lump in my breast. I just knew it couldn't be cancer because, after all, I was the fittest, healthiest person I knew. Although I was then 47, I was running marathons and had been a daily runner for 14 years. Lean and fit, I'd given up red meat, eating only what I then thought was a very healthy diet.

When I heard the words, "infiltrating ductal carcinoma," a wild panic seized me. I wanted to scream, "No, wait a minute; wait just a darn minute — I can't have cancer! I'm a marathoner, for Pete's sake!" The doctor showed me the pathology report and then a sinking feeling came over me, my knees got weak, and my head started swimming. I could barely hear the doctor's words. Something about more surgery, then chemo, then radiation, then more tests.

Then I thought back even further — to high school days back in the 1950s when I took up swimming and diving as my sport. Since I was the only female on the team, I was, by definition, the "best," which I needed to hear because I was also usually the "last" when racing with the boys. From there, I entered the state diving championships and won a gold medal. My dreams went soaring! I was going to enter the Olympics and be an Olympic champion!

After graduating from high school and getting started in college, I found that between my studies and the full-time job required to pay my way through college, there was little time to train. Then I decided that, after all, most kids have seemingly unattainable dreams of being a champion athlete, a movie star, or president, but day-to-day working and studying are usually the stark reality. My dream slowly faded over the years into a vague, nearly forgotten past.

Things started to change back in 1968; while walking past a bookstand, I saw the book *Aerobics*, by Kenneth Cooper, M.D. Thumbing through it, I saw that running as an exercise has many benefits. In fact, for every ailment I had, it seemed that running was the answer, from head to toe, insomnia to flat feet!

I bought the book and devoured it in one sitting, finishing about 2:00 a.m. I fell asleep determined to start a running program. To my surprise, I woke up at

5:00 a.m., an hour earlier than my usual wake-up time. Jumping out of bed, I scrambled through my closet, found my old tennis shoes, and threw on a pair of shorts and an old T-shirt. Out the front door and down the street I went, but it felt really weird. I was thankful that nobody in the neighborhood was awake, because I certainly would have been embarrassed!

I continued down to the end of my street, a half mile away. Since I was then only 33 years old, there hadn't been too much deterioration of my body. I was feeling pretty smug as I turned back, thinking that if I ran all the way home, I would have run a whole mile! When I got back, I jumped in the swimming pool, swam a couple of laps, and then rushed to get to work. I felt so energized and fit and strong that I decided to do this routine every morning — which I did!

I followed this routine for several years, extending the turnaround point as I got stronger. One day, someone mentioned a race coming up, a three-mile "Turkey Trot." I thought that might be fun; plus, I was anxious to see how I'd do after nearly five years of running.

As I toed the start line, I looked around and saw nothing but guys. "Wow," I thought, "I'm the only female here — just like the high school swim team." This was now 1973, when road racing was just getting started with very few men and even fewer women. Since all I had to do was finish, I came home with a gold medal, an automatic first place since there was no female competition. I was pretty excited about my new road-racing career and trained to go farther and faster. Later, as women started to enter these competitions, there were age divisions. As I got older, I entered older age groups, but I was still winning and racking up gold medals.

The diagnosis of breast cancer just didn't fit and yet, there it was. Then I learned two things that turned my life around. First, that animal foods increase your risk for cancer and, second, that cancer cells thrive in an anaerobic (no oxygen) environment. But, wait just a minute, running was aerobic, so it had to have been the diet that led to my cancer. Working with John McDougall, M.D., who was at that time doing research that linked animal foods to breast cancer, I changed to a low-fat vegan diet. Also at that same time, I saw the 1982 Ironman Triathlon on TV and decided that just in case running wasn't aerobic enough, I would start swimming again and added cycling to be really sure. To give myself a goal, I sent in my application to do the Ironman. Never mind that no woman my age had ever completed one, never mind that I was now a cancer patient. As I trained and got stronger, my goal of becoming an Ironman became a reality. I'd never been so fit in my whole life and here I was in my 50s! Eventually, I completed the Ironman six times.

Then, in 1996, I entered the Senior Olympics in Las Vegas. I figured that I didn't need to worry about the triathlon course because I would just follow the person in front. But once I started — to my great surprise and shock — I was the first out of the water, and first on the course, and I had no one to follow! I panicked as I thought, "Here I am in first place and I'm going to blow it by getting lost." I steadied myself and came up with a strategy: "When in doubt, go straight." My heart settled down, but the anxiety was almost unbearable as I pedaled as fast as I could. I kept waiting for a sign that I was on the right course, and I didn't know if someone would overtake me and cause me to lose first place. But I was also thinking, "What a tremendous coup to beat all the men," so I wasn't about to slow down. I got through both the bike and run course, and, unbelievably to me, I crossed the finish line first overall!

Standing on that stage, I thought about how far-fetched the whole drama was, that here I was at 61 years of age and I'd just won an Olympic gold medal. That taught me to never give up your dreams, even if they are Olympic dreams — Senior Olympic Dreams!

55

Go the Distance

by Michael Milone, Ph.D.

Michael Milone, Ph.D., is a research psychologist in New Mexico. At 61, he runs at least one marathon a month, and he runs, swims, bikes, and skis — every chance he gets.

Don't stop reading because you think a marathon is impossible. It's not as hard as you think! Those rumors about Phedippides dying, in 490 B.C., after running 25 miles from Marathon to Athens to announce the Greek victory over the Persians, are probably untrue. Thousands of people complete a marathon each month, and most live to tell about it. And, most of them do it again.

Running a marathon in your 60s is probably easier now than when you were half that age. After six decades, we are more patient and pensive than younger runners. The ability to train for — and complete — a marathon requires far more mental strength than physical conditioning. Don't get me wrong; you've got to put in a lot of miles. It's your head that will get you there, though.

Nonrunners and runners who have not yet done a marathon overestimate the physical effort involved. I was just as guilty of this misunderstanding before I ran my first one. Although I was in great shape and regularly ran half-marathons, as well as shorter races, I had convinced myself that my knees would never hold up for 26.2 miles, and I wanted to preserve them for as long as I could.

What prompted me to undertake my first marathon was a base human instinct: competition. My wife completed a marathon before I did. What made this even more embarrassing was that my wife isn't a runner. She went to a marathon as support for a friend, who was running her first. When my wife saw the variety of people crossing the finish line — hardly the super-athletes she had envisioned — she thought, "I can do this." A year later, she completed the Flying Pig Marathon in Cincinnati, Ohio.

Realizing that I couldn't live with my wife, or myself, unless I ran a marathon, I gritted my teeth and, four months later, ran my first marathon.

It became addictive. I now try to run one a month, and I do shorter races and triathlons in between. This may sound daunting, but it's not. I have friends who have run a marathon a week, for a year. Others do back-to-back races, running a marathon on Saturday and another on Sunday. For those who have completely lost their minds, there's the Labor Day Trifecta.

Now that you've started to think about doing a marathon, you should consider who your training partners are going to be. Unless you are a Zen master, you're going to need some companionship during your training, and on race day. You don't need a trainer, just some racing buddies. Perhaps you can talk some of your friends or family into it, or you can hook up with a local group. If you aren't a serious runner, don't worry. Local running groups are as interested in partying as they are in running. Sure, there are usually a few "burners" in every club but, for the most part, the members are just people who love to run. There are far more slow runners than fast ones, and the people in the back of the pack have a lot more fun than the early finishers.

A third way to find training buddies is to join a fund-raising group, such as Team in Training (sponsored by the Leukemia & Lymphoma Society). TNT, as the group is called, will help you train and will support you on race day. Lots of other organizations also use marathons as fund-raisers. If you don't mind hitting up your friends and family for donations, a fund-raising group is probably the best way to prepare for and complete your first marathon. You'll meet great people, have an easier time training, and be doing an enormous amount of good through your fund-raising. In some marathons (London is the best example), the majority of the participants are raising funds, and race organizers reserve slots for these groups.

In addition to training buddies, you will need a training schedule. This will be the easiest part. There are countless books and Web sites devoted to running or walking a marathon. Scout a few of them and choose a program that matches your goals, the time you have available to train, and your personal style. If you hook up with TNT or another group, they will provide you with a training program.

Preparing for a marathon doesn't have to be

intimidating. You'll have to be dedicated and consistent, but you can make it an enjoyable part of your life. Training buddies always make it easier, and music or a radio is virtually a requirement. Nothing makes the miles go by more quickly than listening to your favorite music, radio station, or book while you run or walk. Some people like to take their music or book to a marathon, but many enjoy chatting with the other participants and listening to the sounds of the crowd. Some of the most interesting people I've ever met have been running alongside me in a marathon.

This brings up the issue of the race you choose for your first marathon. Most people choose one of two options: a race that's convenient and usually local, or one that's big and spectacular. A local race is usually cheaper and more convenient, but you might end up with stretches that are pretty lonely. (That's the importance of training buddies who participate with you.) A big and spectacular race will have support throughout the course, there will always be people around you, and the crowds will provide you with the enthusiasm to get through the tough miles.

If you think that I'm guiding you toward a big race as

your first marathon, you're right. In addition to the advantages I've mentioned, the big races are held in wonderful venues. The huge marathons like Chicago, Honolulu, London, New York, Paris, San Diego, or Walt Disney World are exhilarating. Everyone remembers his or her first marathon, and when the memory includes something like crossing London Tower Bridge or getting a hug from Mickey Mouse, it will bring you joy for the rest of your life!

56

Write That Novel!

by Stephanie Cowell

Stephanie Cowell fell in love with writing and music at an early age. By 20 she had twice won prizes in national story contests. She sang as a high soprano in opera and as an international balladeer; formed a singing ensemble and a chamber opera company; and produced concerts and Elizabethan festivals. She is the author of *Nicholas Cooke: Actor, Soldier, Physician, Priest*; *The Physician of London* (American Book Award 1996); *The Players: A Novel of the Young Shakespeare*; and *Marrying Mozart*. Cowell retired from an office job to write novels full-time in her 60s, which resulted in *Claude & Camille: A Novel of Monet*. Her next novel is about Elizabeth Barrett Browning. Cowell's work has been translated into several languages. She is married and has two grown sons. Her Web site is www.stephaniecowell.com.

"I've always wanted to write a novel," people tell me wherever I go. "I have such wonderful ideas! If only I had enough time." Well, if that's been your dream, now that you are retired, you can make it come true.

Writing novels is ideal for older people. Laura Ingalls Wilder, the beloved author of the *Little House on the Prairie* series, didn't publish her first book until she was well into her 60s. Helen Hooven Santmyer was 88 when she published her bestselling novel "...*And Ladies of the Club.*" Creators of series novels (Patrick O'Brian and Ellis Peters) continued writing into their 80s. You can set your own hours and you can show up for work in your pajamas. You can take a four-hour lunch if you want.

Writing a novel requires only a computer (or pad and pen), your imagination, and a handful of hours a week. There are many how-to books to help you along. You don't need to take classes but you can. What you *will* need above all is a desire to tell your story. "Writing is a great patience," the novelist Flaubert said while he was writing *Madame Bovary.*

A novel can seem a bit daunting when you consider the complexity of the characters and plot and structure, but the truth is, every novel begins with one sentence. Even *War and Peace* or *The Da Vinci Code.* A 300-page novel is written one word at a time. At first you'll think you can never write so much, but as you become more involved with the story, you'll find that your imagination takes off and a whole world begins to spill forth, one that only you can write. And that is one of the most important reasons to do it: no one can tell the story you love just the way you can. No one else has lived your life.

Writers who began publishing early and continued well into their older years include Doris Lessing, who won the Nobel Prize at the age of 88, and the sensual French writer Colette, author of *Cheri*. There are Nadine Gordimer, Grace Paley, Philip Roth, and the amazing Henry Roth, who published his first novel, *Call It Sleep*, at 28 and the next one 60 years later. Rather a long wait for his public!

Now in my mid-60s, I am on the verge of publishing my sixth novel. Since childhood, I wanted to write stories that would express what I wasn't always able to in my life. In my 40s, two characters from Edwardian England appeared like shadows in my mind; I would wake to the murmur of their voices. Friends challenged me to make them into a novel and I did, albeit a very rough one. I was possessed to make it better; I lent copies of drafts to anyone who would be so kind as to read it. (Some people said, "You have a gift!" and others said, "What is this thing?")

At that time, I had an office job. Like the mystery writer Mary Higgins Clark in her early career, I got up very early to write before the needs of family and work. I lived in two worlds: the world I was creating and my real one. I used every extra minute to write or research the historical periods in which my novels were set. I haunted libraries during my lunch hour and edited printouts on the subway. I was utterly determined to write something worth publishing. After completing four novels in seven years, I sold one to a major publisher. A few years ago, I retired from my job and became a full-time novelist.

You will find that the writing life is a rich journey. Through letters and e-mails, you will make friends with other writers. They can bolster your confidence when you feel your book just isn't working (even the most successful novelists have times when they would like to throw it all in the garbage). You can also read each others' scenes and drafts. Form a writers' support group. I had one that met every month for 10 years. The members are still my close friends and we still share our work.

If you wish, your new writing life will include travel to your choice of writers' conferences or fascinating places to research your book. Imagine yourself sitting by the Grand Canal taking notes on your characters!

People always ask me how long it takes to write a novel. Some people take three months and some take 10 years. Set yourself a schedule; make appointments with yourself to write and take them as seriously as you would anything else. Some people write at night; others in the early morning. Some take days off and others never do. There will be periods of great joy and periods of disillusionment, which is true for all of us. There are times when you'll be so tired that you'll need to walk away just to give your mind a rest. Fifteen hours a week is a good amount of time for some people, 10 for others.

Mary Higgins Clark, now 84, works several hours a day. Writing a novel opens up whole new worlds, both within you and around you. Whatever story you want to tell, write it with all the wisdom and love of your life — describe the things that interest you most, the periods you want to bring to life, the people and the memories you want to share, the things you wish had happened, the things you wish had not.

Section 7: Go for It!

Write one sentence and then go on until you have put on paper the story you have within you.

But above all, write that novel!

57

Tool-Belt Spirituality

by Sally W. Paradysz

Sally W. Paradysz was born, raised, and earned her degree in the Berkshires of New England. Today she writes memoir and fiction in the cabin she built in the woods of her Bucks County, Pennsylvania home, and it is from there that she pens a weekly blog for those searching for a breath of calm. As an advocate for the self-empowerment of women, she draws upon her own life experiences, bringing the world a message of healing, love, and inspiration. Ordained into the ministry of the Assembly of the Word, founded in Quakertown, Pennsylvania, Paradysz has provided spiritual counseling and ministerial assistance for more than two decades. She is the mother of three and grandmother of eight, and along with her housemate, Melanie, lives with their two flamboyant Maine Coon cats, Kiva and Kodi, who love their life in the woods.

Retirement is not ending a career. It is learning to redefine your self.

Every life has a story and every story has a lesson. My life's lesson was that I had to let go of my structured existence long enough to find out where I truly belonged.

Growing up as a woodsman's daughter in the Berkshires of New England, I worked side by side with my dad in a perfect dance between master sawyer and lumberwoman. I felt alive, equal, needed. Back then, my restrictions were defined by the measure of my own strength and will. Physically, I was not as strong as my father, so he taught me the art of leverage, and with a cant hook my force became his counterpoint. I tucked that skill in my tool belt. Together, we walked the forest daily. Trees to be cut were selected carefully and with reverence. It was here that my interest in mysticism began to take seed.

As a young woman of 21, tool belt aside, I put all of my energy, all of myself, into being a wife, mom, and coworker, accepting the limitations of those roles. Raising children is the ultimate sacrifice of self, a decision you make out of love, and I did so eagerly. I allowed my personal interests, occupations, and spirituality to become secondary. When my children married and had families of their own, I chose to retire from those limitations. A burning ember inside me was screaming to get out. I was tired of living in a controlled environment, having my every role defined by others telling me what I must or could not do. I had always been passionate about my spiritual growth, so from that moment forward I lived within the heart of my soul. Letting go of borders brought back my true *self*.

By taking courses from the Network of Victim Assistance in Doylestown, Pennsylvania, I added a new tool to my belt. I became an advocate, working for the self-empowerment of women, and I have advised victimized women on a hotline, and in hospitals and police stations. I've also provided spiritual counseling and ministerial assistance to members of my church. I feel blessed to freely offer them my help. As I set down my list of priorities, I understand how little wealth I need to live a rich life.

At 60, I decided to follow the dream of building my own house in the woods. Pushing back against society's limitations, I worked hard alongside my crazy-cool, opera-singing contractor, who showed up every morning before seven. All the while, I lived in a tiny tool shed with no heat, no water, and no indoor plumbing. I relearned how to become integrated into the natural world that surrounded me. Red-tailed hawks built a nest in the iron stanchion of the power lines nearby. Daily I compared my life to theirs as they made a home, had a family, and watched with excitement, yet sadness, as their fledglings left the nest. The gift that came with this unique experience was embracing my spirituality. It was time to share my passion with others.

At 65, I constructed a writing cabin at the edge of my forest. It sits proudly on its stone foundation, one that I built with my own hands. It is a tranquil setting, and one I love. In this small cottage I can be still and uncomplicated, enabling me to live in clarity and conscious choice. It's here that I developed my skills to write memoir and fiction. And from here that I've counseled those who come to me carrying anxieties caused by the world's pressures. If intention determines outcome, I've created an environment to help them find peace.

Looking out my cabin window, I realize how much I have committed myself to respect. When I let go of limitations, I found a new life of compassion for all beings, whether they be other people or the animals that live on my land. I possessed these feelings when I was younger, but I can now dedicate more attention to them.

I feel blessed with my three beloved children and eight grandchildren. Our journey together is not over, and it's my hope to help them all develop a sense of their own spirituality. I want to impart to them that, during the course of their lives, it does not matter who is right, but that they bring a piece of the light of themselves to every moment — that life is a gift and love connects us all.

Retirement is something we all look forward to, and there is so much freedom and excitement in the various choices awaiting us. For me, I live to hear the music of God's finest whispers in every birdsong, and I am thankful for each day. I experience euphoria by living without being limited by the judgment of others. During the Equinox, I asked myself, "What does this time mean for me?" My answer was that all life, including mine, is one and the same in the eyes of our Creator. It is a reminder that we all have a finite time on this earth, and it is important for me to balance the gifts I've been given, to take responsibility for the space I hold here, and to use my tools to make a difference within it. I feel that now I am giving in a way that enriches — rather than depletes — me.

This earth will live on after I leave. Have I lived my teaching? If my reply is no, then I must challenge myself to do better. Each morning after meditation I have the opportunity to start again, to define by example what it means to be giving from myself in a way that enhances rather than diminishes. For it is at this juncture that I hope to work even harder with what I've learned, for the Greater Good.

What is genuine and what is lasting is who you are. No one can take that away.

58

Be Inspired Night and Day

by Greg Mort

Greg Mort grew up during the height of the Space Race between Russia and the United States. When he was five, his father took him outside to gaze into a star-filled sky to observe Sputnik, the world's first artificial satellite. That event helped shape his life's vocation and avocation. Now, as a professional artist with works in prominent museum and private collections around the world, Mort melds his passions for art and astronomy into one flowing stream.

nspiration. I am convinced that the very fabric of art and astronomy are embedded in our DNA, part and parcel of the human existence. Have you felt this pull also? When you view a sculpture or painting, do you feel yourself strangely bonded to its artist? And, like me, as you gaze at the night sky, do you get the feeling that it claims *you* for its own?

I'll admit that I'm a passionate seeker of beauty, in both art and the stars. For as long as I can remember, painting and astronomy have sustained and fulfilled me on a daily basis. In fact, I'll wager that if you locked me up in a room that lacked paints and windows, it wouldn't take long for my soul to go into painful withdrawal.

I submit that artistic yearning and expression evolve from our need to bond with this great Universe, to leave a bit of our essence behind when we ourselves join the stars. I paint to leave a bit of my soul, guided by the creative pulse of the artists who came before me.

Let me put this another way. Who among us is not lured by the sight and warmth of a fire? And why, after 40,000 generations, do we still feel a kind of hypnotic quality in those flames? The reason is simple. It's because for 99 percent of our history we huddled around those fires. They represented security, light, heat, a way of staying alive. Though our technological advances long ago made this way of keeping warm obsolete, the fascination of the flames remains.

Why? Because they are part of our collective human experience. The same holds true for human creativity. Like those early artists who felt the inclination to draw on cave walls, I also feel the need to capture what I see.

It's been said that artists are born, not made. Perhaps. Perhaps not. Maybe I paint better than you because I've given myself permission to plug into the creative pulse I feel so strongly.

Were you, perhaps, told by your parents that you weren't creative, or did you take it to heart when a well-meaning art "teacher" cautioned you to "stay within the lines"? It's a good thing Walt Disney ignored the teacher who admonished him that flowers shouldn't have faces! Disney gave the world considerable beauty and inspiration — because he drew from the fount of universal creativity.

Now that you're in your 60s, old enough to care little about what others think, and old enough to make your own rules, perhaps you'll give yourself permission to create your own art.

The good news is that artistic expression is not difficult to access once you decide to tap into it. And once you connect, you'll become an addict like me. You won't be able to resist the infusion of invigoration and renewal, the high of birthing a form that only you can create.

A visit to an art museum is a great place to discover

artistic inspiration. There, you can connect with various forms of art on its most intimate terms. Perhaps it is the texture and glisten of the paint, or the dimensionality of the piece that grabs my soul, but I leave itching to paint.

The world's great monuments also serve to inspire. To behold the menagerie of animals drawn on the cave walls of Lascaux is to bear witness to some of the most expressive works ever created by human hands. The paintings tell of the spirit of the hunt, but the quarry represents much more than food. The paintings were a means of connecting with the spirit of the creatures themselves. In essence, the artists were paying homage to Earth's bounty while praising the majesty of the Universe.

Similarly, the sheer size and mass of the stone markers at Stonehenge, the mysterious astronomical sculpture on the Salisbury plain in England, attest to the ancients' desire to connect with the stars, a universe so expansive it makes the massive stones seem like pebbles.

On the days when I need a huge infusion of creative inspiration, however, I head for the stars. There are few things I savor more than venturing from the glare of city lights to slip into the refuge of a moonless night sky. Shhhhh, I tell my soul: be still, be quiet.

There, under the canopy of a starry blanket, I am overcome, humbled, by the vastness of the Universe. Yet, I am comforted by the knowledge that I am tied to it. I sigh in contentment, knowing I have seen this lightshow before — perhaps even a million years ago. Listening, I can distinctly make out the tick-tock of the clockwork of the heavens and its ever-flowing creative hum.

When I view original art, be it a painting or a starry star, I instinctively feel close to its maker.

This knowledge awaits you, too. If you're in the city, jump into your car this very night and drive until you find a perfect spot clear enough for stargazing. Or, jump on a plane and take in the majesty of Stonehenge, perhaps on the longest day of the year, as the sun rises between two of the monoliths. Your soul will connect with the Universe; its beauty will bring you home.

59

Breathe In, Breathe Out

by Beryl Bender Birch

Beryl Bender Birch graduated from Syracuse University with a degree in English and philosophy. She has been an avid student of classical yoga and the study of consciousness since 1971, and her work merges the traditions of Classical Raja Yoga, Vedanta, Buddhism, and Jainism. Through her school, The Hard & The Soft Yoga Institute, she has been teaching classical yoga and training yoga teachers as "spiritual revolutionaries" for over 35 years. She is the author of the best-selling books, *Power Yoga* and *Beyond Power Yoga*, as well as *Boomer Yoga*, and she is also the founder of the Give Back Yoga Foundation.

Do yoga! Whether you are retired or not, don't wait. Start today!! We all have bucket lists: ride the Trans-Siberian railroad, hike the Brooks Range in Alaska, sit by Walden Pond and write a poem, or learn to speak Spanish. But this all presupposes that we stay healthy into our 70s, 80s, and beyond, so that we have time to do all the things we want to do after we retire. And nothing I know of can keep you all-around healthy like the practice of yoga and meditation.

The word "yoga" in general parlance is often, but incorrectly, understood to be synonymous with the word "asana," which is simply the *portion* of yoga that involves the practice of the yoga postures. People say, "I'm going to practice yoga," and others think basically they are going to exercise. But classical yoga is actually an eight-limbed path that includes everything from practicing right living (truthfulness, non-greediness, non-harming, etc.), to keeping the body fit and flexible, to mindful breathing and meditation. The *methodology* of yoga, which starts with the yoga postures, leads to the *experience* of yoga, which is the experience of complete boundlessness and joyfulness, and the recognition that *everything in this universe is connected.*

Every aspect of the practice of yoga is designed to lead us from gross levels of awareness (focusing on the body) to more subtle levels (focusing on the mind and spirit) through the process of learning to pay attention to the present moment. This, from a health standpoint, automatically increases our body awareness, reduces anxious thoughts about the past or future, and increases our ability to enjoy the moment. For this reason, the various practices found in different schools of yoga and meditation are contributing to the revolution going on in medicine. It used to be that the only people who knew about the health benefits of mind-body practices like yoga were those who were on some kind of a spiritual path. But now doctors and scientists are investigating yoga to see how it can benefit our physical and mental health. New studies and data are showing and confirming what the yogis have always known: that the mind can heal the body and that yoga (including meditation) can help relieve stress, depression, insomnia, and anxiety disorders, lower cardiovascular risks, and improve the quality of life for sufferers of chronic disease. Yoga can also help you to relieve stress in your life, maintain or regain good health, and bring you greater peace of mind and a deeper sense of joy and happiness — starting today!

Our body's reaction to stress is to turn on what is called the *fight or flight* response. This involves our sympathetic nervous system releasing "stress hormones," like adrenaline and cortisol, to get us ready to fight or run away from threatening danger. These hormones are not necessarily "bad"; they have been a lifesaving part of our body's response to stress and have kept us in existence as a species. But once the stress has passed, it is equally important that our body's functions return to normal. However, in our current high-stress culture, we tend to stay "stressed out" a good part of the time, and we don't give ourselves a chance to settle down. Consequently, we end up in a state of chronic stress.

Continuous stress, no matter what the source, takes its toll on our health. It weakens the immune system, turns on inflammation, and speeds up aging. To maintain wellness, as the yogis know, it can be vitally helpful to learn to *consciously* turn on the *relaxation response* — which is the polar opposite of the *fight or flight* response. The *relaxation response* calms us down — it slows our metabolism, heart rate, blood pressure, and rate of breathing; it calms our brain activity and increases our ability to pay attention and make decisions. How can we do this? We can start a yoga practice; if we can breathe, we can begin the practice of yoga.

The foundation of all yoga, meditation, and stress-management programs is mindfulness, which simply means learning to pay attention and "be present" with whatever is going on now, no matter what it is. Although we want to learn to be mindful in everyday life, an example of a formal yoga practice might be to focus your attention for a period of time on your alignment while in a yoga posture, or on the breath, a word or prayer, a subtle sense perception, the sounds around you, or most anything else that elicits a calm and peaceful state of mind. It is this process of learning to pay attention to *this* moment that quiets the mind and turns on the relaxation response. As we get better in this practice of *paying attention*, we learn to notice more quickly when we get distracted, lose focus, and start "thinking" about something, and we see how that can lead to anxiety or distress.

Our first startling realization is that we can actually *watch* our thoughts, and next we realize that we really have a choice as to how far our mind goes — we can be *here* or we can wander off into dreamland. And since "here" and "now" is the only place we can ever really be, then the only other choice if we aren't *present* is to be *absent*. And if we are absent, where are we? Well, we're not here and we then miss out on this wonderful panorama of experiences that life offers us. And now that we are retired, we don't want to miss out on a single moment of our remaining days on this earth.

So, along with everything else you want to do, start

yoga. It's good for your health, your head, and your heart. Find a class — it might be movement, breathing, or meditation, or all three. Breathe in, breathe out.

Master Your Look

by Sharon Haver

Sharon Haver, founder and editor in chief of the online fashion magazine, FocusOnStyle.com, turned her love of shopping and style into an expansive 25-year career in the glamour industry as a New York–based photography fashion stylist, Scripps Howard News Service syndicated newswire columnist, and on-air television/radio fashion expert and spokesperson. She is every woman's fashion, style, and beauty guru and believes in effortless can-do chic. Haver is frequently quoted and seen in national media, including the *Los Angeles Times*, *Real Simple* magazine, ELLE magazine, iVillage, USA *Today*, *New York Daily News*, *Chicago Sun-Times*, and on Martha Stewart Radio, CNN. com Living, CNBC.com, and Lifetime TV Online. Haver starred as herself in her own national commercial for Macy's. She lives in New York City with her husband, son, and toy poodle.

Some may think that fashion is wasted on the (very) young. Trends come and go. Taking risks is merely a part of any day. Money, well, more will come later, so why not spend away now?

Fashion is fun. It's frivolous and it's something that

should not be taken too seriously or you will miss the nuance, the thrill, the charge of it all.

But style, oh style, that mysterious combination of what works and what is magic on the wearer . . . what flatters as it shields and shows you only in your best and most effortless light — the perfection that is unique to you. That kind of style is something that comes with time, with experimentation, with understanding your body (and its changes) and your lifestyle.

It's your time to shine.

But just as you master your look, your life adjusts or your figure repositions itself. Then what? Are years of honing, years of perfecting, down the drain?

Hell, no.

Every modification can lead to a better, more fine-tuned, more vital version of you. For some who have lived a life within the confines of a professional dress code, it may mean that now is the time to finally take that fashion risk to discover the new, more stylish, sophisticated, and even younger-looking you. It's time to take the challenge to celebrate you in the purest form of your style — where you are in control, and, most important, where you don't look old.

Not Too Old, Not Too Young

Nothing saps the spirit more than looking dated, dreary, and dowdy. So many women get carried away with their sudden, newfound freedom from dress codes that they resort to wild and crazy extremes for sudden self-expression.

Avoid the classic "mutton dressed as lamb" look by trying to pull off teenybopper styles in a sour effort to dress young. No matter how youthful you think you look, there's no greater slap of truth than bright daylight. Accept sophistication and tear yourself away from fads and overexposure.

Don't forget that style is more than just what you wear, but *how* you present yourself as a whole. By now, you have evolved into the person you are, and it's a matter of keeping up appearances to maintain your visual vitality. Style is what's realistic for you, for your lifestyle, and for the shape that you are in today. At my Web site FocusOnStyle.com, I share my tips on how to master ageless and timeless can-do chic. Sit up, take notice, and be proud, but most important, take control of your chic style.

Beauty Starts Here

Never forget to moisturize your skin and condition your hair. It seems so easy, almost second nature. Sadly, many instantly add years to their appearance by having lifeless hair and dull skin. The right moisturizer, antiaging products, and regular deep hair conditioning are easy steps to help you look fresh and vital.

Avoid getting stuck in the same dated hairstyle that you had in your high school yearbook photo or one that is over-dyed and dry in an attempt to cover the gray. Look at some social media avatars of boomers for instant visual proof of what being trapped in a hair time warp looks like!

This is not the time to forgo makeup but to understand how a light touch can compensate for the loss of facial volume that comes with age. Apply a bit of blush to flush the cheeks and a tint of lipgloss; lightly define your brows; and use some cosmetic help to make your eyes sparkle so they don't look drained.

Avoid crazy makeup trends and experimenting with glitter, goop, and heavy-handedness that accentuate wrinkles. Keep makeup dewy and natural by highlighting your best features.

When It Comes to What You Wear

Keep the theatrics down and the sophistication up. If you were not one who could pull off being showy in your youth, it's probably not the best time to start now. Looking effortless is the key to looking chic. Clean lines, well-executed silhouettes, and the best quality that you can afford in investment pieces will always look chic.

You have probably amassed a fantastic collection of clothes by now. Rethink how you wear them to better suit your new life. Mix and match different combinations. Think outside of your comfort zone and shop your closet for new and different ways to wear what you already have.

When you do go shopping, stick to classic styles with some design details that aren't boring. You may want to save by buying very inexpensive clothing, but avoid cheap and trendy items. Nothing beats a good sale to find the best for less.

Solids, particularly neutrals with a pop of either primary or muted color, provide a very sophisticated look for women of a certain age and don't come with a built-in style expiration date. Monochromatic separates with added texture for interest are best.

Prints, oh prints. I have no idea why the misses department is flooded with either garish or dipsy prints. Somewhere, there is an evil fashionista who thinks that women over 50 want to drown themselves in the most hideous prints, patterns, and embellishments imaginable. Resist the urge to succumb to fugly clothes that will age you.

Don't show too much, but do strut what you have with style. After a certain age, you may still have a fantastic figure, toned legs, and a bountiful bustline. Just because you've still got it doesn't mean it looks appropriate to bust it out all over. It's better to have clothes that graze the body instead of being clingy. Necklines that reveal just a bit of skin are more flattering than those that overexpose.

When it comes to hemlines, err on the side of sophistication — don't go too short. Use discretion in selecting silhouettes.

Don't try too hard. Trust your own sense of style. Kick back and remember, it's all about can-do chic!

61

Don't Take Retirement Sitting Down: Stand Up and Make Everyone Laugh Instead

by Leigh Anne Jasheway

Leigh Anne Jasheway is a comedy writer, performer, and corporate comic. She won the 2003 Erma Bombeck Award for Humor Writing as well as number of other comedy-writing awards. She has 17 published books, including *Not Guilty by Reason of Menopause* and *Confessions of a Semi-Natural Woman*. Her humorous columns have been published in dozens of major publications, including *Family Circle Magazine*, *Funny Times*, and the *Los Angeles Times*. You can read her funny stuff or get more information about taking an online class at her Web site, www.accidentalcomic.com.

Two years ago, a 78-year-old woman with a walker ambled onto a comedy stage in Eugene, Oregon. Her gray hair had been dyed fluorescent pink and spiked into a mohawk of sorts. As she reached the microphone, she stared into the spotlight and began her set: "Hi, I'm Patrice. I've never had much luck with men. Or women. People really. But I do like small dogs." The crowd erupted in laughter. Patrice grinned widely, knowing she was, as they say in the 'biz, "killing."

Patrice is one of nearly 900 students who have taken my stand-up comedy class in the past 17 years. Most, like Patrice, harbor a desire to get on a stage, share their life story with an audience, and make people laugh.

Because the class I teach is offered in the evenings as part of the continuing education curriculum, I get many students who are retirees (not to mention, many who wish they were). During the 10-week class, we work together to apply the principles of comedy writing to each student's life, and at graduation they perform an eight-to-ten-minute-long set, usually in front of a sold-out audience of friends and family. It's always fun and often a life-changing experience. No one has ever had vegetables thrown at them.

Chances are, you already bring laughter into the lives of the people you know, and it probably makes you happy to be able to do so. But most people are more frightened of being onstage, trying to make people laugh, than they are of having a root canal in a backless paper gown while stuck in an elevator with a heavy metal band.

There is no more empowering, eye-opening, and just-plain-fun legal pursuit you can choose than stand-up comedy. It's one thing to make your friends and family giggle, but the ability to make a roomful of complete strangers laugh while sharing stories from your life is a feeling you will never forget. In fact, once you try it, you may never want to stop, no matter how much someone pays you.

When I had a stroke, they took away my driver's license. But they forgot to take away my forklift license. If you need anything moved, that's my forklift in the handicapped zone.
— John, retiree and former student

Laughter can reduce blood pressure and heart rate, improve your immune system, circulate your blood and oxygen more effectively to all your organs and muscles, burn calories, tone your abs, reduce tension headaches, increase endorphins, lower blood sugar spikes, increase good cholesterol, and make you feel better about life in general. All of that without any serious side effects! What prescription drug can make that kind of claim?

When we leave the house, we turn the stereo on for the dogs.

If they've been bad dogs, we turn on country music.

— Judy, retiree and former student

Learning to write and perform comedy has benefits all its own. It can:

- Help you move past your fears.

- Teach you not to take everything in life so seriously.

- Change whining into joke-writing.

- Enhance memory and cognition.

- Broaden your circle of friends to include more funny people.

One thing about dating on the Internet — you learn to dislike someone without ever meeting them.

— Susan, retiree and former student

The best way to try your hand at stand-up comedy is to find a comedy class. A class gives you structure for learning the tools and techniques of comedy writing; it also will help build your confidence so that when you do get up onstage, you are not overwhelmed by nerves (and if you are, you know how to channel them into being funny). Many large and even midsized cities have comedy classes available either through community colleges or other educational venues. Search for comedy classes online and see what pops up nearby. Like me, some instructors also teach long-distance classes for people who don't have access to nearby instruction.

You can also create your own comedy homeschooling classes by reading some good books, giving yourself comedy-writing homework, attending open mic nights to see performances in action, and then getting up onstage yourself. If you'd like to try this approach, some books I use and recommend include: *Comic Insights: The Art of Stand-Up Comedy* by Franklyn Ajaye, *The Comic Toolbox* by John Vorhaus, *Zen and the Art of Stand-Up Comedy* by Jay Sankey, and my own book, *Yoga for Your Funny Bone.* When you watch other local comedians perform, pay attention to how they use their voices, their faces, and their bodies — comedy is not like public speaking; you don't hide behind a lectern, show a few slides, and pray that the audience can hear you over the snoring . . . some of which is yours! Also, study techniques of using a microphone — you can't be a successful comedian if you can't be heard by the audience.

If you're looking for something that challenges your mind and body, helps you make new friends, and gives you more confidence in everything you do, stand-up comedy may be just the ticket. Not to mention that you'll laugh hard and get healthier to boot. What's not to love?

62

Traveling with Purpose

by Char Matejovsky

Char Matejovsky split her career between academic publishing and working with the Westar Institute, a nonprofit that she and her husband created. A former *au pair, assistante d'anglais* at a *lycée* in France, and exchange student to Mexico, she has a French degree from the University of Montana and a French Language Certificate from the Sorbonne. Her first book, *Stones & Bones*, a short history of evolution for children, was published in 2007. A second is in production. In 2004 she received the Outstanding Achievement in Songwriting Award (for lyrics) from the Great American Song Contest. She lives in Seattle.

G *olf*? Nope.

Bridge? Nuh, uh.

Belly dancing? You gotta be kidding!

Travel? Yeah, sure, but on a shoestring?

Practically everyone I know plans to spend their retirement traveling. But seeing the same old sites, fracturing French, and garbling German, well, it ain't what it's cracked up to be. It's easy to find oneself sidelined, alone, and even lonely. What's more, on my budget, we're probably not talking extended stays in 5-star hotels or vacation rentals. And I'm too old for youth hostels. Still, the idea of traveling until I drop has a firm grip on my imagination, and problems are nothing more than unsolved challenges, or so I'm told.

In addition, there's the reality that traveling, for traveling's sake, is just, well, traveling. It's fast food for the brain. I want it to be nourishing. Slow food, if you like. And for that you need a purpose, something that draws you into the lands you visit. For ideas, I cast back to my childhood. I passed the time, during long car rides on family vacations, playing an imaginary keyboard. Listening past my brother's alternate lyrics ("redder than tail lights were her lips"), I scored each radio offering in my head. It was exciting and deeply satisfying.

A demanding career and overactive life put music on the back burner, which was then shut off, you might say. In anticipation of retirement, I rekindled that interest with a class in digital music production. That put not just a keyboard but the whole orchestra at my fingertips. So, it occurred to me, why not write a piece of music for each country I visit? One that echoes the distinctive sounds of that culture, like Smetana did in *Má vlast*. He was Czech. I'm sort of Czech. He'd be a good role model, I reasoned. I gave the idea a trial run on a trip to New Zealand, with a piece inspired by the song of a native bird, the Tui. It was also composed during a long ride, on the train from Wellington to Auckland, but in this case the keyboard, on my laptop, was real. The experience, once again, was exciting and deeply satisfying.

So purpose firmly in hand, what about those challenges? What can be done to turn my dreams into realities?

The first challenge — finding affordable housing abroad. Solution: swap houses. To optimize the pool of potential exchange partners, I would need to replace my suburban home (and its high-maintenance yard) with an efficient urban loft in easy reach of public transportation. Then, I can throw that loft up for grabs on the home exchange market.

Next up — meeting people. My solution: teach. English,

that is. Realizing yet another dream of my youth, I would dust off my B.A., find a good online course, and get certified to teach English as a foreign language. After all, though I haven't done it in decades, I was trained to teach French. This can't be all that different, can it? (Except maybe that my English is a lot better than my French.) The beauty of it is not only that I'd be meeting people but that they would actually want to speak English. No more fractured sentences. At least, not mine.

Sounds easy, right? It isn't. Not at all.

To start with, trekking up and down the hills of Wellington quickly turned my legs to rubber. So getting into shape will be the first hurdle. Then there's the issue of inertia. A paycheck is a good motivator. No paycheck, not so much motivation. Add to that a Netflix account, and you can imagine how time flies. And that's kind of the point. Time is flying. If I'm to see the world in the years that remain, there can be no more putting it off. And if that's not motivation enough . . .

63

Wildlife Adventure

by Bernadette Heath

Bernadette Heath, a photographer and writer, and Janet Webb Farnsworth, a writer, seniors in their own right, teamed up to find adventure, live that adventure, and inspire armchair seniors to become hikers, horse packers, four-wheel-drive vagabonds, and wildlife enthusiasts. They are the coauthors of *Grandma Needs a Four-Wheel Drive: Adventure Travel for Seniors* and *Rock Art Along the Way*. In addition, they have created a Web page, www.grandmaneedsafour-wheeldrive.com, and blog, www.adventurousseniors.blogspot, which encourage additional excursions. Heath is the author of *Arizona Impressions*, *Grand Canyon Impressions*, and *Phoenix Impressions*.

Congratulations. If you spent some of your retirement bonus on a new digital camera, adventure is in your future. Wildlife abounds in our national parks, wildlife refuges, and wilderness areas. The best news is, viewing and photographing wildlife is an exciting activity that can be successfully done from the front seat of your car.

Now that you are retired, traveling in the off-season may be easier and quite rewarding. In late fall and early winter, animals that live in the mountains are pushed down into valleys and river bottoms, searching for food. Grass is first exposed along the plowed shoulders of roads. Last February, on the North Fork of the Shoshone River in Cody, Wyoming, there was a herd of bighorn sheep on the blacktop of State Highway 20 that stopped traffic from both directions. Using a 24–85mm zoom lens, I was able to shoot out of the truck's rolled-down window and get sharp, full-frame images. The thrill of experiencing wildlife up close and personal is like reliving your retirement party all over again.

At the entrance of the North Rim of the Grand Canyon National Park, there is a large herd of runaway buffalo from a neighboring buffalo/cattle ranch. By stopping at the pull-over area, you will have the opportunity to photograph a buffalo herd, and also learn how visitors from other countries say the word "buffalo." The best prospect for seeing buffalo in winter or summer is Yellowstone National Park. While you are there, check out the wolf packs, grizzly bears, elk herds, and moose.

A bear encounter in the wild can be a hair-raising experience. Using grizzly bear spray and a full combat outfit *might* be a safe way to approach a bear habitat, but a less hazardous alternative is to visit one of several privately owned rescue parks, where photographing black bears can be done safely from your vehicle. Bearizona in Williams, Arizona, has 13 rescued bears, plus a large variety of other animals from all over the United States. An early-morning drive-through, when they are feeding, will produce more activity. Remember that these animals are retired, like us, so they enjoy frequent naps. This park requires you to have your windows up, so non-tinted windows are best for photography. Another option for photographing a range of wildlife is the Out of Africa Wildlife Park in Camp Verde, Arizona, where you can ride on a Serengeti Safari bus among African animals like giraffes and zebras, plus warthogs, lions, and a bear or two.

Birding offers a wide range of possibilities for photographing, and it is so popular that most states provide online information on their best birding areas. Padre Island at Corpus Christi, Texas, is proud of its White-tailed Kite. Its neighbor to the east, Galveston, has boardwalks from which the Roseate Spoonbill, with the help of a long lens, can be photographed. At a visitor center, ask for "The Great Texas Coastal Birding Trail" map, created by the Texas Department of Tourism.

Both the Atlantic and Pacific coastlines have an abundance of shorebirds and other varieties for viewing and photographing. But if you don't live or travel near the water, there are still exciting birding opportunities. Kofa National Wildlife Refuge, in southwest Arizona, lists 185 bird species, with 25 of them documented as nesting on the refuge. Cibola National Wildlife Refuge, between Arizona and California, lists 288 species. Keep in mind that most birding in southern Arizona is done in the winter.

My most exciting encounter when photographing birds was on Mary Lake Road in Flagstaff, Arizona, in the winter. It was a migration of Bald Eagles and the whole family was there — four generations. In one frame alone, there were seven eagles. If you travel the gravel roads around Lake Superior, Wisconsin, nests of returning pairs of eagles can be located and watched from a respectful distance, so as not to disturb the family.

As long as we're discussing birds, consider the rare California Condor, reintroduced at the Vermilion Cliffs in Arizona. The easiest shooting, with the best chance of success, is at Bright Angel Lodge, on the South Rim of the Grand Canyon National Park, where the condors return about an hour before sunset.

If you want images of sea wildlife, check out the coastal tidal pools along Washington's Olympic National Park at low tide. Or you could visit the Feiro Marine Life Center in the small town of Port Angeles, Washington. Run by volunteers, students, and staff, its entrance is marked by a dramatic sculpture of an octopus spreading its tentacles across a huge rock. Inside, you'll find a real octopus, along with sea horses, starfish, eels, jellyfish, sea urchins, and other saltwater creatures. Another great location is New Mexico's Albuquerque Aquarium, where you can eat lunch while watching huge sea turtles, sharks, eels, and jellyfish swim right by your table, on the other side of the glass. Increase the ISO on your camera and shoot away.

Whatever your destination, here are some helpful tips to remember when photographing wildlife: Being kissed by a dolphin and running your camera at the same time could mean a wet camera. Taking your camera into an enclosed butterfly house can fog up your lens. (I try to use the fog for effect until things clear up.) On the road, when photographing a rattlesnake or other critter that you do not want to approach, set your camera's timer on a 3- to 5-second delay and drop the camera out of your vehicle's window, hanging onto it, using either the cord or a monopod. When using your vehicle as a tripod, turn off the motor.

Think of your vehicle as a transportable moving blind that gives you an opportunity to view and photograph wild animals in their natural environment. This way, adventure is just around the next bend in the road.

64

How to Plan a Round-the-World Trip

by Mahara Sinclaire, M.Ed.

Mahara Sinclaire, M.Ed., and her husband, Ken, have experienced a 35-month odyssey around the world, logging hundreds of thousands of miles as they visited 46 countries. This former musician, college and university instructor, and learning specialist says her desire for adventure, as well as her willingness to change and to reach for new goals, is what sets her apart. She hopes that her new book, *The Laughing Boomer: Retire from Work — Gear Up for Living!*, will give others the motivation to live their dreams. Her Web site is www. laughingboomer.com.

D o the Taj Mahal, the ruins of Tikal, or a charming European city capture your imagination? Travel often tops the list of lifetime goals. However, while some retirees take a few trips, many people never fulfill their dream of traveling. Travel can be overwhelming to contemplate. You may get distracted by life or think it is too expensive. But you can find a way to realize your dream, be it an around-the-world trip, a cruise, or a season in the sun.

Are You a "Go-Go, Go-Slow, or No-Go"?

A good time for long-term travel is right after finishing work. Other people haven't claimed your time, and you haven't established a slowed-down mode of living, volunteer commitments, or golf lessons yet. Reflect on life's next steps from a sunny beach paradise, not at your kitchen table.

People are generally healthier and stronger at 60 than 90. At 60, you might enjoy adventure travel with a myriad of conditions, and accept longer travel days or unusual food. Arrive at the doorsteps of Paris in your 90s, but visit exotic countries now.

Perhaps most important is for you to recognize that time slips away. We do not have control over some health aspects as we age. Your valuable early retirement years are the time for active travel.

We started our retirement and traveled for three years, full-time, to 46 countries. Had we waited, we would not have traveled as we did. Climbing the Petra ruins, riding camels in Egypt, canoeing down the Amazon, snorkeling in the Galapagos, sleeping in the Sahara desert, bird-watching in the Peruvian jungles, and walking the tiger reserves in India are challenging physically.

Note that travel insurance increases substantially as you age — younger retirees get better rates. Unfortunately, after a heart attack and a stroke, my husband cannot fly for six months and is uninsurable. How bad is that? We are not traveling.

Freeing up Funds Is a Major Key to Travel

Downsize your home and possessions. It took us a full six months to finish renovation projects, and to sell our house and excess stuff. We moved the basics into storage. We had no payments for utilities, cars, mortgage, house insurance, or property taxes. For three years, our fixed costs were our medical insurance and less than $300 per month for our storage locker. Depending on your lifestyle and country, maintaining a home can cost between $10,000 and $30,000 per year. You can see a lot of the world for that price.

Big-Picture Planning

Set a date and go for it. The momentum will move you forward. Do your big-picture planning first. Get an atlas or put a world map on your wall, and go wild picking and planning a route.

Understand your personal style. Travel reveals the true you. Do you fancy adventure travel, packaged tours, independent travel, or serendipitous encounters? Would you feel uncomfortable without a plan? We've done all styles, and each has its benefits.

From this big-picture planning, you can estimate your expenses. Do some general searches to find local costs of living, as well as the best weather options for each destination. One-year, round-the-world trips can run from $15,000 (most likely a backpacking expedition) to $150,000. Rough out the year, balancing your time between expensive and more affordable areas. North America, Europe, and "world-class" cities are costly. If you spend most of your time in other regions, $30,000 to $40,000 can work. Costs can be similar to staying home. Modify your plans to fit your time and money.

Transportation will be a large expense. Compare round-the-world trips from the airline alliances — OneWorld, Star Alliance, and SkyTeam — with repositioning cruises in the "shoulder seasons" of spring and fall. For example, we cruised from Lisbon to São Paulo for

15 days, for $500 each. Find interesting transportation options within each country. Try everything, from camel riding to buses and second-class trains.

A sample-year itinerary is six months in Southeast Asia and the East, or South and Central America; two months in Western Europe; and the balance of time in Eastern Europe or North America. Spend several months on one continent, rather than rush-rush-rushing around the world.

Become comfortable with online technology and information sites. Round-the-world travelers generally book a few months in advance, but not the full year. Even if you book your major tickets through an agency, you will book some things online, such as first-night hotels. Many people book their side trips and longer-term accommodations when they arrive.

Assemble the electronics you will need: camera, notebook or tablet, music player, portable hard drive, and connectivity devices. Your current cell phone access probably will not be available. Arrange your computer phone accounts at home and work out snags. Plan online photo storage needs, as cloud computing is not worldwide.

Have credit cards from both Visa and MasterCard, and cover the various interbank systems. Open an account with an international bank, a national bank, and a credit union account. Know your PIN verification codes and phone numbers for all your credit and debit cards. Usage of security PIN numbers and signatures is evolving. Direct your post office box provider (ours is UPS) to courier your mail as needed.

Remember that you will become a traveler, not a tourist. Let the country and its people speak to you. Read about and research areas linked to your personal interests; for example, if you enjoy art, then focus on major galleries. If environmental issues are important to you, learn and connect with others worldwide who share this same concern.

Traveling the world has been a highlight of my life. I appreciate my own country, Canada, more than I ever imagined. Travel has connected me with dozens of friends from around the globe. World events have a greater context now because I have seen the struggles others experience. Of course, I want to do more, give more, and live life to the fullest. However, most important to me is that I have lived my dream. Live yours.

65

Traveling Top Speed at 65 and Above

by Doris Gallan

Doris Gallan is the Baby Boomer Travel Coach and author of *The Boomers' Guide to Going Abroad to Travel | Live | Give | Learn*. Her travel tips booklets discuss topics including: finding authenticity through activities, staying healthy and safe, eating well, packing light, uncovering alternative accommodations, and saving money. Gallan has traveled around the world twice, journeying to all seven continents, visiting over 50 countries, and living in five. She is also a consultant to the travel and tourism industry, providing advice on creating and marketing products for her fellow baby boomers. Her free "Daily Travel Tips" and weekly newsletter are available at www.BabyBoomersTraveling.com.

If a man for whatever reason has the opportunity to lead an extraordinary life, he has no right to keep it to himself. — Jacques-Yves Cousteau

Study after study has shown that the number-one priority within boomers' retirement plans is traveling. Older adults place travel before family, health, financial security, and religion in their lists of needs, desires, and concerns. As much as 40 percent of boomers — those born between 1946 and 1964 — say travel and vacations take precedence in their lives.

Among all of the elements in the world that can make your life extraordinary, you have the most power and opportunity to achieve the dream of travel. You can plan, research, and book practically everything for travel yourself (or with the help of professionals), and, by doing so, set the stage to have the amazing life you've always desired.

Where does this power and opportunity come from? When you attain a certain age, you have more knowledge and experience than ever to help you figure out what you want and how to get it. Consider taking advantage of these hard-earned traits to go abroad to travel, live, give, and learn.

The Boomer Advantage

People turning age 65, beginning in 2011 and continuing through 2028, are part of the enormous baby boomer generation. There are about 78 million boomers in the United States — and guess what? Along with you, about 77.9 million boomers have discovered they've got a lot more leisure time and money for travel than ever. They're taking trips, exploring the possibility of living abroad, and going on volunteer and learning vacations.

You may be thinking, "How can they do that?" We're bombarded by news about not saving enough for retirement, older worker job-loss statistics, and the forever-impending Social Security bankruptcy. Is it possible for people to travel or live abroad, even in light of these dire predictions? Yes!

In my travels to more than 50 countries on all seven continents, I've encountered boomers and seniors enjoying a few weeks' vacation on tropical beaches, taking a year off to travel around the world, looking for retirement homes in Third World countries, volunteering in orphanages and animal preserves, and teaching English as a foreign language in Asia.

Getting Back to Our Travel Roots

Travel is nothing new to boomers. In fact, we're the most traveled generation in history. We started young in the back of the family station wagon, sustained by Pop-Tarts, Tang, transistor radios, and spot-the-license-plate games.

After high school or college, many of us backpacked on $5 a day through Europe or followed the hippie trail in Asia. Later, we earned tens of thousands of air miles on business trips, and often used them to fly our families across oceans on vacations.

Our travel habits aren't likely to change now that we're entering the life stage where career and children don't take up all our time and money. People in their 50s and 60s continue looking for opportunities to keep active, both physically and mentally.

For many of us, that means taking trips that offer new knowledge and experiences, allow us to rediscover old interests and latent talents, and give us the chance to make a difference in the world in ways that are new to us.

Hitting the Road, Air, Seas . . .

If you haven't traveled much, I recommend you start easy by seeing more of your own country, or venturing to countries where the culture, language, and customs are similar. Once comfortable with your initial forays, expand your horizons to other parts of your country, or go abroad where greater differences lead to bigger adventures. Once these journeys feel too tame, take a major step and leave the comforts of your culture, language, and ethnicity to go somewhere entirely unfamiliar.

On the other hand, you may already have seen a good part of the world and believe there isn't much left to discover. If so, it's time to open yourself to travels of a different kind. Instead of returning to the usual locations, consider visiting Third World countries. Try traveling independently of tour groups by doing your own planning and making your own arrangements — and save thousands of dollars. You might volunteer for a project on another continent — orphanages, community rebuilding, animal rescue; there are thousands of programs available. Going abroad to study a language, skill, or craft offers opportunities to immerse yourself in a new culture and become part of a community.

Maybe you'll join the ranks of retirees who move to foreign countries for a year or indefinitely, in part because the cost of living is so much lower than in most of North America. Not ready for retirement, but looking to start a new career? Consider a stint teaching abroad, which may provide you with a great sense of satisfaction. At this stage of life, you have so much to offer from your decades of life and work experience.

It Doesn't Take Much

The thousands of travelers I've encountered shared a common desire for continuous learning, a need for authentic experiences, and a deep concern for their role in leaving the world a better place. That and a little sense of adventure are all that's needed to travel the world.

About the Editor

Mark Evan Chimsky is editor in chief of the book division of Sellers Publishing, an independent publishing company based in South Portland, Maine. For eight years, he ran his own editorial consulting business. Previously he was executive editor and editorial director of Harper San Francisco and headed the paperback divisions at Little, Brown and Macmillan. In addition, he was on the faculty of New York University's Center for Publishing, and for three years he served as the director of the book section of NYU's Summer Publishing Institute. He has edited a number of best-selling books, including Johnny Cash's memoir, *Cash*, and he has worked with such notable authors as Melody Beattie, Arthur Hertzberg, Beryl Bender Birch, and Robert Coles. He was also project manager on Billy Graham's *New York Times* best-selling memoir, *Just As I Am*. He conceived of the long-running series, *The Best American Erotica*, which was compiled by Susie Bright, and he was the first editor to reissue the works of celebrated novelist Dawn Powell. His editorial achievements have been noted in *Vanity Fair*, the *Nation*, and *Publishers Weekly*. He is an award-winning poet whose poetry and essays have appeared in JAMA (the Journal of the American Medical Association), *Three Rivers Poetry Journal*, and *Mississippi Review*. For Sellers Publishing, he has developed and compiled *Creating a Business You'll Love*, *Creating a Meal You'll Love*, *Creating a Marriage You'll Love*, and *Creating a Life You'll Love*, which won the silver in ForeWord's 2009 Book of the Year Awards (self-help category).

About the Associate Project Editor

Renee Rooks Cooley, Associate Project Editor, is a freelance editor and proofreader based in South Portland, Maine. She is a *summa cum laude* graduate and valedictorian of Emerson College, where she received a BFA in Creative Writing. A former staff proofreader for Houghton Mifflin's school division, Renee began her publishing career as a longtime poetry screener and office manager for *Ploughshares* magazine. Her poetry has appeared in literary publications, including the *Washington Square Review*.

Credits

"Don't Let Retirement Steal Your Bliss!" © 2012 Fairview Imprints LLC; "Rewire® Early and Often" © 2007 Jeri Sedlar and Rick Miners; "Retire 'Retirement' . . . Build Your 'Life Portfolio' Instead" © 2012 New Directions, Inc.; "New Models for Success" © 2012 David C. Borchard, Ed.D., NCC; "Five Keys to a Creative Retirement: Even When This Means Continuing to Work" © 2012 Ronald J. Manheimer, Ph.D.; "Will You Pass or Flunk Retirement?" © 2012 Nancy K. Schlossberg, Ed.D.; "Women 50+ Know: How to Redefine Retirement" © 2012 VibrantNation Online U.S.; "Change the World" © 2011 Andrew Carle; A Cartoon © 2007 Mort Gerberg; "What Happy Retirees Know" © 2012 Sydney Lagier; "65 and Lucky" © 2012 Bill Roiter, Ed.D.; "Trump Fear with Purpose" © 2012 Mary Lloyd; "There's More to Retirement Planning Than Finances" © 2012 Mike Bonacorsi; "Retirement Is an Opportunity to Rethink Your Life and Do Something Different" © 2012 Susan E. Kersley; "Live to 100!"© 2006 Dr. Thomas T. Perls, reprinted from 60 Things to Do When You Turn 60. Reprinted with permission of the author; "Positive Aging — Old Is the New Young" © 2012 LoveBeingRetired; "Expand Your Social Circle – Face to Face" © 2012 Susan RoAne; "Career Women and Retirement: 6 Important Tips" © 2012 Helen Dennis and Bernice Bratter; "Women and Retirement: Inventory Your Successes" © 2012 Attract Your Ideal Retirement; "Choices" © 2012 Elizabeth Doucet; "Budget for 100 Years" © 2006 Anna M. Rappaport, reprinted from 60 Things to Do When You Turn 60. Reprinted with permission of the author; "Seven Financial Rules for Retirees" © 2012 Mark Cussen, CFP, CMFC; "What to Look for in Financial Advisers" © 2012 Jim Yih; "Managing Retirement Wealth without a Crystal Ball" © 2012 Julie Jason; "Four Emotions to Manage When Maintaining Your Nest Egg" © 2012 Aaron W. Smith, RFC; "The Best Years of Our Lives" © 2012 The Carter Center; "Enrich Your Life: Push Back Against the Box" © 2012 Robert M. Lowry; "A New Dimension to Our Lives" © 2012 William S. Birnbaum; "It's Not Where You've Been, But Where You're Going" © 2012 Rick Koca; "Embrace Life" © 2012 Pamela Good; "For LGBT Retirees and Their Allies, Volunteer Opportunities Abound!" © 2011 Services and Advocacy for GLBT Elders; "Retire and ReServe: Because You Should" © 2012 Mary S. Bleiberg; "The Encore Career" © 2012 50+ Digital LLC; "What's Next? Finding Your Dream Job in Retirement" © 2011 Kerry Hannon; "How to Turn a Hobby into Retirement Income" © 2012 Joan Jones; "Starting a Home-Based Business in Retirement" © 2012 Art Koff; "Six Ways to Get Paid to Travel During